HUMAN RESOURCES
for Results

The Right Person for the Right Job

JEANNE GOODRICH and PAULA M. SINGER

for the

PUBLIC LIBRARY ASSOCIATION

AMERICAN LIBRARY ASSOCIATION

Chicago   2007

Printed on 50-pound white offset, a pH-neutral stock, and bound in 10-point coated cover stock by McNaughton & Gunn.

The paper used in this publication meets the minimum requirements of American National Standard for Information Sciences—Permanence of Paper for Printed Library Materials, ANSI Z39.48-1992. ∞

Library of Congress Cataloging-in-Publication Data

Goodrich, Jeanne.
    Human resources for results : the right person for the right job / Jeanne Goodrich and Paula M. Singer for the Public Library Association.
    p.   cm. — (PLA results series)
    Includes index.
    ISBN-13: 978-0-8389-3570-5 (alk. paper)
    ISBN-10: 0-8389-3570-2 (alk. paper)
    1. Public libraries—Personnel management. 2. Public libraries—United States—Personnel management. 3. Strategic planning. I. Singer, Paula M. II. Public Library Association. III. Title.
    Z682.G67 2007
    023—dc22   2007015743

ISBN-13: 978-0-8389-3570-5
ISBN-10: 0-8389-3570-2

Printed in the United States of America

11 10 09 08 07   5 4 3 2 1

To our partners,
Michael Pearlman and
Jacqueline Ehlis, for
your unfailing support
and confidence in us

Contents

Figures

Acknowledgments

The authors thank Sandra Nelson and June Garcia for their guidance and support for this book as well as for the entire Results series. The series has become a highly regarded set of books designed to provide library managers with practical tools that they can use to plan and deliver responsive library services to their communities. We're pleased that we've been able to contribute to this effort.

We also thank our wonderful book review committee: Joan Airoldi, Karen Avenick, Irene Blalock, Josephine Bryant, Faye Clow, Bill Dietz, June Garcia, Consuelo Hernandez, Jill Jean, Sara Laughlin, Jean Mantegna, Sandra Nelson, Chuck Sherrill, Lydia Tinder, Julaine Warner, and Lynn Wheeler. The committee members provided invaluable feedback to us based on their collective experience and insight as public library managers and HR professionals. We know that the book is much stronger and more relevant to public libraries of all sizes because of their assistance.

And finally, we thank the public library community and our many public library clients. Working with you all has informed our practice, expanded our thinking, and kept us grounded in reality.

Introduction

Managing a public library has always been hard work, and it is becoming even more difficult under the twin pressures of restricted public funding and rapid change. The Public Library Association (PLA) plays a major role in providing the tools and training required to "enhance the development and effectiveness of public librarians and public library services."[1] During the past seven years, the PLA has provided support for the development of the Results series, a family of management publications that are being used by library managers, staff, and boards around the country to manage the libraries in their communities more effectively. The seven publications in the Results series that are available in 2007 are

> *The New Planning for Results: A Streamlined Approach*[2]
>
> *Managing for Results: Effective Resource Allocation for Public Libraries*[3]
>
> *Staffing for Results: A Guide to Working Smarter*[4]
>
> *Creating Policies for Results: From Chaos to Clarity*[5]
>
> *Technology for Results: Developing Service-Based Plans*[6]
>
> *Demonstrating Results: Using Outcome Measurement in Your Library*[7]
>
> *Managing Facilities for Results: Optimizing Space for Services*[8]

These publications provide a fully integrated approach to planning and resource allocation, an approach that is focused on creating change—on *results*. The underlying assumptions in all of the books in the Results series are the same:

> Excellence must be defined locally. It is a result of providing library services that match community needs, interests, and priorities.
>
> Excellence does not require unlimited resources. It occurs when available resources are allocated in ways that support library priorities.
>
> Excellence is a moving target. The best decision-making model is "estimate, implement, check, and adjust"—and then "estimate, implement, check, and adjust again."

The Results Publications

All of the books in the Results series are intended to be used with *The New Planning for Results: A Streamlined Approach.*⁹ *The New Planning for Results* describes a library planning process that is focused on creating an actual blueprint for change rather than a beautifully printed plan for your office shelf. As you can see in the diagram of the *Planning for Results* model shown in figure 1, the process starts by looking at the community the library serves in order to identify what needs to happen to improve the quality of life for all of the community's residents. Once the community's needs have been established, library planners look for ways the library can collaborate with other government services and not-for-profit agencies to help meet those needs. That, in turn, provides the information required to establish the library's service priorities.

FIGURE 1
Planning for Results Model

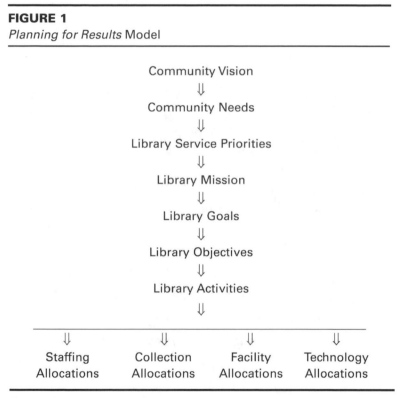

Source: Sandra Nelson and June Garcia, *Creating Policies for Results: From Chaos to Clarity* (Chicago: American Library Association, 2003), xii.

The planning process includes significant participation by community residents who represent all of the constituencies served by the library: parents and children; working adults and seniors; business people and civic leaders; students and educators; the various racial, ethnic, and religious groups in your community; government and not-for-profit leaders; and all of the other groups that together create your unique community. By involving all of these groups in your planning process, you ensure that the services you provide are really what community residents want—and not what you or your staff or board think (or wish) that they want.

Because *The New Planning for Results* is focused on identifying and implementing the activities that will help library managers and staff to accomplish community-based goals and objectives, the decisions that are made are sure to affect every part of the library's operations. Every library manager, every library staff member, and every library board member are going to have to become used to the idea of continuously evaluating all of the services and programs the library currently provides and all of the policies that support those services in the context of the library's identified priorities—and then be willing to make any changes that are necessary. Changes don't happen because we want them to or hope they will. Changes only happen when we do things differently.

There's Always a Plan

All of the books in the Results series assume that libraries have current strategic plans with clearly defined service priorities that were developed using *The New Planning for Results.* However, a strategic plan is not the only way that library staff and board members can determine service priorities. Some libraries participate in city or county strategic planning processes. Others choose to develop annual goals and objectives rather than a multiyear plan. Yet others develop goals and objectives for individual units, for branches, or for specific programs or services. A library's annual budget sets and reflects service priorities for the upcoming year whether a library has engaged in a formal planning process or not. Any process used to determine the library's service priorities, goals, or objectives can serve as the starting point for the tools and techniques described in this book.

However, it is important to understand that this book is about allocating—and reallocating—your human resources (HR) to support the library's priorities and not about determining what those priorities should be. This book is predicated on the assumption that you have done work to determine the direction your library is attempting to go and that you know what your priorities are. Since this book is about using HR functions strategically to assist you in achieving your goals, you need to know what those goals are and have some methodologies in place to measure your progress in attaining them. Once you know what you want to accomplish and have a way of measuring your accomplishments, you can start using the techniques described in this book.

What This Book Is—and Isn't

Human Resources for Results: The Right Person for the Right Job is not designed to be a comprehensive human resources textbook. This book will focus on how library managers can use various HR functions to support the goals and service priorities that their strategic planning process has identified. For example, this book addresses job analysis and the development of job descriptions not simply as part of the day-to-day activities of an HR department, personnel analyst, or busy manager, but as activities that are vitally important to the achievement of the library's goals and objectives. Carrying out these activities in an efficient manner and keeping monthly statistics is not the point: identifying the knowledge, skills, abilities, and competencies needed to achieve the library's service objectives is the goal. Therefore, senior managers and HR practitioners must collaborate to be sure that the library has the means to carry out its plan of service.

There are a number of basic textbooks on human resources management written for library managers, managers in the public sector, and managers in general. If you are completely unfamiliar with the basics of HR management, reading a few books and taking an introductory class would be very helpful to provide a basic orientation. While these are not a substitute for formal education, you will gain some familiarity with the terms and concepts of the field.

Employment law specialists frequently provide one- or two-day seminars, usually referencing applicable state laws and current issues that impact employers, such as sexual harassment, the Fair Labor Standards Act (exempt/nonexempt status), background checking, the Family Medical Leave Act, and state family leave legislation. After you feel you have the basics down, it would be worthwhile to take one of these courses every year or two as a way to keep updated, particularly on issues that could carry substantial liability costs for your library if ignored.

You might also want to consider joining the Society for Human Resource Management, which is the world's largest association dedicated to human resource management; or the International Public Management Association for Human Resources, which is an organization that represents the interests of HR professionals at the federal, state, and local levels of government. Both maintain websites that provide a wide range of information on all human resource management topics.

Definitions

Before you begin to read this book and use it to make decisions about the way you will use your human resources, it will be helpful if you understand how some basic terms are used. Every public library is a little different. At some libraries people refer to "branches," in others the term is "agencies," and in still others the term for departments and branches is "units." Some libraries have "central" libraries; others have "main" libraries. There are libraries that report to governing boards and libraries that are units of the government entity that funds them. They may or may not have advisory boards. These differences can be confusing as the reader looks for his or her reality reflected in the terms and examples used in library literature. A list of terms and their meaning *in this book* follows. Definitions appear within each chapter as needed to introduce new terms.

> *Branch.* A separate facility.
>
> *Central library.* The largest library facility, usually in a downtown area; referred to as the main library in some places.
>
> *Department.* A unit within a single facility.
>
> *Library.* The entire organizational entity and its units.
>
> *Manager.* A generic term that refers to the staff member or members who are responsible for resource allocation in a particular area; in some libraries the "manager" is actually a team of staff members.
>
> *Team.* A group of staff members brought together to work on a specific project or program; often includes members from different departments and with different job classifications.
>
> *Unit.* A term used to refer to individual library departments and branches, if any.

In addition, terms used within the processes described in this book include the following.

Goal. The benefit your community (or a target population within your community) will receive because the library provides a specific service response.

Objective. The way the library will measure its progress toward reaching a goal.

Activity. A grouping of specific tasks that the library will carry out to achieve its goals and objectives. Activities result in an output of things done or services delivered.

Steps. Sequential actions completed in the performance of an activity.

Project. A temporary endeavor requiring concerted effort by one or more people to initiate or implement an activity.

Using *Human Resources for Results* in Your Library

This book is different from many of the other books in the Results series because it describes a number of possible projects rather than a process that would be followed, beginning to end, throughout the book. You don't have to do everything written about in this book. You also don't have to undertake the projects in any specific order, although there is a logical order to how they are presented and how they interrelate with each other. You can instead decide which projects it is necessary to undertake to help you and your library achieve your strategic goals. Each library's path will be different.

Human Resources for Results provides a number of processes to help you and your employees deploy human resources strategically in your library. Each chapter (with the exception of chapter 1) provides tasks and steps to follow in order to complete the project described (see figure 2).

How to Use This Book

This book includes two tools that will help you understand the concepts in the book and use those concepts to address issues in your own library. The first is a series of examples that allow you to see how the staff in the fictional Tree County Library would use the information in this book to make HR decisions in their library. The second is a series of workforms to help you collect the data you need to make informed HR decisions.

Tree County Library

The Tree County Library was introduced in *Staffing for Results* and has appeared in several Results publications. Tree County is a mythical county somewhere in the United States with a countywide population of 400,000 people. The library serves the residents of Tree County with seven branches and has a governing board. You will see examples using the Tree County Library throughout this book.

FIGURE 2

Tasks and Steps in the *Human Resources for Results* Process

Task 1: Assess Required Staff Resources

    Step 1.1: Plan the project

    Step 1.2: Determine what you need

    Step 1.3: Determine what you have

    Step 1.4: Identify the gap

    Step 1.5: Develop a plan to bridge the gap

    Step 1.6: Implement the plan

Task 2: Describe the Job

    Step 2.1: Plan the project

    Step 2.2: Job analysis

    Step 2.3: Write job descriptions

    Step 2.4: Obtain approval and communicate

Task 3: Identify the Right Person for the Right Job

    Step 3.1: Plan the project

    Step 3.2: Recruit candidates

    Step 3.3: Screen and test candidates

    Step 3.4: Interview candidates

    Step 3.5: Check references and make job offer

Task 4: Develop and Implement a Performance Management System

    Step 4.1: Review or develop a performance management system

    Step 4.2: Manage and monitor a performance management system

    Step 4.3: Develop individual performance plans

    Step 4.4: Monitor and coach individuals

    Step 4.5: Evaluate and rate individuals

    Step 4.6: Plan for the next cycle

Task 5: Develop and Implement a Retention Plan

    Step 5.1: Plan the project

    Step 5.2: Understand workforce needs and expectations

    Step 5.3: Create the culture

    Step 5.4: Define expectations

    Step 5.5: Provide training

    Step 5.6: Build commitment

Workforms

This book includes twelve workforms to help you collect and organize information. It is very unlikely that any library will use all of the workforms that are provided. Each workform starts with a purpose statement. Before you decide to use a workform, read the purpose statement carefully. If the purpose does not meet your need, don't use that workform, or feel free to revise it. Samples of portions of some of the completed workforms are shown in the figures to illustrate information and show the results of action in an example. Blank workforms are located at the end of the book. All of the workforms in this book are also available in electronic format for download in Microsoft Word format at www.elearnlibraries.com. The electronic format of the workforms makes it easy for you to expand the space available on them for entering data and to adapt the workforms for your own needs.

In addition to providing a mechanism to collect and organize the data you will need during the *Human Resources for Results* processes, the workforms will help you and your staff avoid thinking up all kinds of data that "would be nice to have," a common statement in the world of librarianship—and one that can get you stuck forever in the data collection phase of a project. You will want to collect only data that is essential for the decision-making process.

Used separately or taken as a whole, these tools will provide you with new ways to use human resource management functions and techniques to accomplish your library's goals and objectives in order to provide your community with the library services it wants and needs.

Notes

1. Public Library Association Mission Statement, http://www.pla.org/factsheet.html.
2. Sandra Nelson, *The New Planning for Results: A Streamlined Approach* (Chicago: American Library Association, 2001).
3. Sandra Nelson, Ellen Altman, and Diane Mayo, *Managing for Results: Effective Resource Allocation for Public Libraries* (Chicago: American Library Association, 2000).
4. Diane Mayo and Jeanne Goodrich, *Staffing for Results: A Guide to Working Smarter* (Chicago: American Library Association, 2002).
5. Sandra Nelson and June Garcia, *Creating Policies for Results: From Chaos to Clarity* (Chicago: American Library Association, 2003).
6. Diane Mayo, *Technology for Results: Developing Service-Based Plans* (Chicago: American Library Association, 2005).
7. Rhea Rubin, *Demonstrating Results: Using Outcome Measurement in Your Library* (Chicago: American Library Association, 2006).
8. Cheryl Bryan, *Managing Facilities for Results: Optimizing Space for Services* (Chicago: American Library Association, 2007).
9. Nelson, *The New Planning for Results*.

Chapter 1

Strategic Human Resources

Human resources management is about people, the people who work in our public libraries. Public libraries can't deliver services without employees. The largest portion (ranging from 55 to 85 percent) of a public library's operating budget goes to personnel costs: salaries, wages, and benefits. And the operating budget is only part of the investment. Managing people is time- and energy-consuming. As with so much else we do, it's easy to get bogged down in the details of HR work and forget that our sizable investment in people is for a greater purpose: providing the services the library's customers need and deserve.

Understanding the issues and engaging in the tasks identified in *Human Resources for Results* will lead to creating a library that has high and sustained

- productivity
- quality of work life
- competitive advantage
- workforce adaptability
- results!

Human resources management is the term now used to describe a number of functions related to the decisions, activities, and processes that must meet the basic needs and support the work performance of employees. This term is designed to underscore the fact that people (human resources as opposed to raw materials—or books!) are a major ingredient for the success of any enterprise, particularly a service organization such as a public library. Terms like *human resources* or *human capital* have replaced the traditional terms *personnel management* or *personnel administration* to indicate that organizations now view their employees as vital investments that must be strategically considered and managed as carefully as any other organizational assets. In fact, most management books will go on at length about the importance of human capital, yet note that many top managers don't think about how critical it is for the success of the organization to have the right people in the right place doing the right things.

As management expert Peter Drucker has written,

> Managers are fond of saying, "Our greatest asset is people." They are fond of repeating the truism that the only real difference between one organization and another is the performance of people. . . . And most managers know perfectly well that of all the resources, people are the least utilized and that little of the human potential of any organization is tapped and put to work. But while managers proclaim that people are their major resource, the traditional approaches to the managing of people do not focus on people as a resource, but as problems, procedures, and costs.[1]

The terms *personnel management* and *personnel administration* have been abandoned because they are thought to be too narrow in scope, concerned primarily with the nuts and bolts of handling paperwork, keeping records, and managing the mechanics of recruitment, testing, selection, performance evaluation, and so on. In fact, Peter Drucker has likened personnel management to mundane household tasks:

> Personnel management is [the] methodical and systematic discharge of all the activities that have to be done where people are employed, especially in large numbers: their selection and employment; training; medical services, the cafeteria, and safety; the administration of wages, salaries and benefits, and many others. Personnel management has to be done. Otherwise there is serious malfunction. But personnel management activities bear the same relationship to managing people as vacuuming the living room and washing the dishes bear to a happy marriage and the bringing up of children. If too many dirty dishes pile up in the sink, the marriage may come apart. But spotless dishes do not by themselves contribute a great deal to wedded bliss or to close and happy relationships with one's children. These are hygiene factors. If neglected, they cause trouble. They should be taken for granted.[2]

When human resources management, in theory and practice—as well as in name—replaced the traditional personnel management, it brought new status, focus, and job assignments to practitioners as well as to the organizations where they worked. HR staff began to add value to the work and employees, not just engage in transactional activities that move paperwork through the process. It was a major leap in the effectiveness of HR activities. The HR field is experiencing another radical change. In recent years we have seen a shift from the HR manager's role as a tactician in implementing organizational objectives to serving as a strategic partner, helping to transform the library.

In the next section, we will elaborate on the basic functions that support effective human resource management. Once we have a grasp of these functions, we will begin to analyze the difference between tactical and strategic human resources—and you'll see why both are needed.

Human Resource Functions

Human resources management is concerned with five basic functions:

Recruitment and retention. Finding, selecting, and hiring the employees you need to get the library's work done, as well as making sure employees want to continue to work for the library

Compensation and benefits. Determining wages, when and how pay increases will be given, and researching and administering benefits, such as health insurance and retirement benefits

Training and development. Making sure that employees receive the training they need to continue to provide the services the library's customers need and want, and that employees continue to grow and develop to advance within the library and to meet the library's needs

Performance management. Designing an effective process that provides coaching and feedback throughout the year; assisting managers with performance appraisals and dealing with substandard job performance

General employee administration/employee relations. Handling payroll and record-keeping, general communications, and events (Staff Day, a blood drive, an employee picnic, etc.); and assuring compliance with applicable federal, state, local, and union laws, policies, and regulations (such as the Fair Labor Standards Act, Family Medical Leave Act, union contract provisions, local personnel rules, safety rules and regulations, etc.)

Every library, regardless of size, must deal with these human resources issues. That means that someone must be responsible for managing these functions. Your library may be large enough to have an HR manager or HR specialists on the staff. Your library may rely upon specialists provided by the city or county of which it is a part. The director, assistant director, department managers, and supervisors may do all or part of the HR work in your library. Or, as is the case in many libraries, you may have to do most or all of the HR tasks yourself. You may have formal training and experience in HR work or, like many, you may have acquired your experience and training through on-the-job experience. No matter what the size of your library, all of this work has to be done . . . there may just be more or less people, time, and expertise on staff.

Throughout the Results series, the tension between *effectiveness* ("doing the right things") and *efficiency* ("doing things right") has been identified as a critical distinction to make when selecting service priorities, making resource allocation decisions, looking at how work is done and staff hours allocated, and developing library policies, procedures, and regulations. It arises here again as we consider the functions of HR management and how these functions can be used strategically to help the library meet its service goals and to capitalize on its expensive and often difficult-to-acquire human resources to meet its goals, carry out its objectives, and deploy its strategic initiatives.

Strategic versus Tactical Human Resources

You've probably heard that *management* is defined as getting things done through people. While HR management encompasses the functions listed previously, the management of employees is the purview of the line managers, the supervisors and managers to whom employees report on a day-to-day basis. There are numerous lists of what line managers do, and thousands of pages have been dedicated to listing the differences between what managers do and what leaders do.[3] For our purposes, we can break down the basic management tasks as

- planning
- goal-setting
- decision-making
- delegating
- supporting employees
- communicating
- controlling to plan (i.e., managing your resources as planned in order to reach your goals)
- evaluating

Unfortunately, many in public libraries think of management primarily as preparing schedules and filling out time sheets. These are routine tasks that must be done, but they fall far short of the higher-level management tasks listed above. Many line managers concern themselves with the daily tasks before them (those that are urgent but not critical) rather than with those which will make a difference in the library's success in the long run.

Traditionally, administration and line managers have viewed the HR function as overhead, a necessary staff function that requires scarce budget resources to fund, but doesn't provide direct services to customers. It is often seen as more of an impediment to providing service than a partner, especially if it is provided outside the library by the city, county, or other organization of which the library is a part.

Human resource management staff can and should be a strong ally with the library's administration and line managers, working proactively with them to provide services, support, and information in ways that make their lives easier and support the library's goals. This is a shift in both the way HR management functions have been carried out and in the way such management has been perceived by others in the library. This shift can be described as moving from a tactical approach to performing HR functions to a strategic approach.

In management as well as combat, tactics relate to small-scale or short-term actions. Strategy, on the other hand, takes a much broader view, over a longer period of time, using a number of different resources. The library's plan of service, if created and written as a strategic plan and not just as a management "to do" list, will be composed of goals and objectives based on community needs. Activities will then be identified and undertaken to accomplish the goals and objectives. Resources (library staff, library collections, buildings and other facilities, and technology) are carefully scrutinized, developed, and deployed to execute the activities selected.

Strategic HR involves using HR functions and activities purposefully in alignment with the library's mission, goals, and objectives. All of the books in the Results series are designed to guide library managers, staff, and board members toward identifying and providing library services that are relevant and responsive to their community. *Change, transition,* and even *transformation* have been watchwords throughout the series. The changing nature of library work, the many real and perceived work pressures felt by library staff and managers, and the reality of increased, multidimensional demands occurring in an environment of severe budget pressures and public antipathy toward public employees, coupled with the ever-faster pace of change, were discussed at length in *Staffing for Results.*[4] In this book, we will show you how HR functions can be used to make some of the transformations needed if libraries are going to thrive in this new environment. (See figure 3.)

All of the activities required by the Results series—planning; allocating resources; measuring, analyzing, and evaluating workload and other library activities; carefully thinking through policy implications and then articulating understandable and defensible policies—require a high-performance workforce. Human capital is not only the largest portion of the library's budget, it's what makes the library very successful—or not.

Turning service goals and objectives into reality requires finding and keeping the right people (possessing the appropriate skills and competencies) who do the right things (providing services and collections that are responsive to the library's community). You must ask yourself the question: "Who are the people that are going to execute our plan and can they do it?"

FIGURE 3
Comparison of Tactical and Strategic Human Resources

Tactical HR	Strategic HR
Internal focus on day-to-day issues such as handling personnel requisitions, payroll, employee records, heath insurance sign-up, employee orientation, planning recognition events, benefits administration, etc.	Takes care of the details (they are important and have to be done) but understands that the library's goals can only be accomplished if the right people with the right skills are doing the right things
Focus on doing things right (efficiency)	Focus on doing the right things (effectiveness)
Maintains the status quo by making only slight refinements for efficiency or cost savings	Looks for and adopts broader innovations and programs
Maintains a reactive posture through offering services and support in response to events	Proactively anticipates events in order to prevent problems or minimize their negative impact

Strategic Human Resource Activities

The shift from tactical to strategic HR in the library involves rethinking both the *way* that HR work is done and the *kind* of HR work that is done. Strategic HR has four major characteristics. First, it is forward-looking, which means that strategic HR looks for ways to forecast or anticipate problems rather than simply react to them. It means further that HR is fully aware of the direction the library is heading and of how HR helps library managers deliver high-quality services. Second, strategic HR is focused on the library's "business problems" rather than only on HR issues, which means that HR is aware of and works to support library goals and objectives. Third, strategic HR participates in increasing workforce productivity and develops and provides key measurements to verify outcomes of productivity efforts. Finally, strategic HR combines the best practices and resources of several HR functions (such as recruitment, compensation and benefits, training, and personnel policy development) to assist the library in achieving its goals.[5]

There are numerous ways to be strategic and proactive in your HR practices. A number of them are listed below. This list should whet your appetite as you begin to identify ways to become a high-performing library that meets, and exceeds, its goals.

Identify people-management practices. You should identify both bad and good people-management practices in your library and reward these accordingly. People management should be defined and identified as a critical expectation of library managers, be discussed during performance reviews, and be linked to pay increases. Many libraries have had the habit of ignoring (or transferring) both poor performers and problem employees. Performance expectations for managers must include addressing and resolving these people-management issues head-on. Poor people managers should be identified and strategies should then be developed to train them, transfer them back to nonsupervisory jobs, or release them if their people-management performance doesn't reach clearly defined, required levels.

Provide metrics. HR staff should also provide good metrics to library managers. They should work with them to develop the list of metrics (turnover rates, time from requisition to working on the job, results of employee climate surveys, training outcomes, etc.) and then provide the information in a timely and consistent manner. Libraries that have developed proficiency in developing these measurements, sharing them with managers, and training managers on how to interpret them are in a far stronger position to identify and deal with trends and to forecast future situations that will impact the library's ability to carry out its service goals.

Develop effective communications. Recognize that the library's supervisors and middle managers are often the delivery system for HR information. Design your communications program and systems accordingly, to be sure the intended messages, policies, and practices get through to employees. You should design communications programs that send messages often, in different media and in a variety of ways to accommodate the many learning styles of your employees. Libraries that use their intranets as a location for HR frequently asked questions have found that their managers and employees are better informed and that fewer routine questions are handled by senior managers or the HR specialists.

Recruit proactively. Develop a "most wanted list" of employees in other libraries and other organizations you'd like to see working in yours. Even if you're experiencing cutbacks or hiring freezes now, you want to be ready when key openings appear. Employment projections suggest that it will become an increasingly competitive hiring environment. You must become much more actively involved in locating and recruiting employees who will bring the skills and qualities you need to your library.

Retain top performers. Re-recruit to keep top-performing employees. In addition to conducting an exit interview to find out why an employee is leaving, conduct periodic climate surveys to find out how current employees feel about their jobs, supervisors, and working conditions. Develop a picture of what keeps employees with your library. Use what you learn to resell your top performers on working for you. Also use what you learn to create new programs and services that employees want and need—and keep you as an employer of choice!

Provide employee challenges. Develop individual learning plans to keep employees challenged with new job assignments, new projects, or advancement opportunities. Many employees don't self-select for advancement, cross-training, or reassignment. Talk with them as part of the performance management process to find out their interests and aspirations and to encourage them to consider new assignments in the library. Help them to manage their careers, thereby helping the library.

Engage in succession planning. From your library's strategic plan, and your knowledge of human resources and library trends, you know what skills and competencies will be needed in the next three to five years. Will the members of your workforce have them? Will they still be there? Will you have the right staff (both technical and leadership), with the right skills, to do the right work when employees leave?

Human Resource Trends

Strategic thinking includes assessing the external environment to observe and understand HR trends that will impact the library's workforce. Forecasters and demographers have identified the following trends that will play an important role in your library's ability to recruit, retain, and motivate high-performing employees. Library administrators, managers, and HR specialists should understand these trends and plan accordingly.[6]

Rise in health care costs. Rising health care costs are the greatest concern among library administrators and HR professionals because they are a huge economic burden and a persistent political issue. Library budgets are directly impacted by the competition for funds as local government budgets strain to find and pay for health care for employees. For the first time, libraries are beginning to or are thinking of shifting a greater percentage of the cost of health care to employees. Most private sector organizations have been doing this for many years. Doing so will have an impact on employee morale. Can your library afford to change its practice? Can it afford not to?

Focus on safety and security. Library managers and employees are dealing with issues of building security, the safety of staff and library users, and the tension between national and global security concerns and the protection of individual liberties. Even the smallest local public library feels the shock waves of global security and international politics because the focus on these issues has real budgetary and political impact, as well as an impact on the cost of utilities, fuel, and the delivery of library materials and supplies. At the personal level, library employees are concerned about job security and whether or not they will have affordable health insurance coverage and retirement benefits.

Use of technology to communicate with employees. Libraries are using a variety of means to communicate with both library customers and employees. Issues involving acceptable use, privacy, and confidentiality, as well as security of information and databases, will continue to come up. Current employees and new hires will be expected to demonstrate comfort and expertise with a wide variety of tools and media.

Growing complexity of legal compliance. Keeping up with employment law and regulations is daunting for HR specialists and is even more of a challenge for libraries that don't have HR specialists to help them. Issues involving immigration and documentation, sexual harassment, safety, family medical leave, wage and hour laws, and age, sexual orientation, and other forms of discrimination abound.

Use of technology to perform transactional HR functions. Library supervisors and staff members have to learn how to prepare time and attendance reports using specialized software. Many employees now obtain information about their benefits, library policies, and union contracts on the library intranet. These new approaches require changes in practices and procedures and additional training, adding to the "change overload" many are experiencing in the workplace.

Preparing for the next wave of retirement and labor shortage. Libraries are seeing retirements, but they are also seeing fewer new jobs open up for new librarians because of the changing nature of library work (e.g., what work really requires an MLS-degreed person?), budget cutbacks, and educational and experience requirements that may not fit the realities of the current hiring market. Thinking strategically about human resources, staffing, and structure will be a necessity as this trend continues to play out.

Use and development of e-learning. Because the environment that library employees find themselves in is changing so rapidly, training—and retraining—is a continuous requirement. Like other kinds of organizations, libraries are looking at using technology to deliver needed training. When done well, e-learning provides effective training at less cost and to a larger number of library staff members. The Public Library Association and other professional and commercial providers are making it possible for staff members to receive interactive, online training at their computers.

Export of U.S. manufacturing jobs to developing countries. Even more than the loss of white-collar jobs, the loss of manufacturing jobs means the loss of good-paying jobs for workers with less formal education, with a resulting impact on the economy and on the stability of middle-class institutions such as publicly funded libraries.

Changing definition of family. The changing definition of the family (children living with grandparents, same-sex couples, households headed up by unmarried couples or a single parent) will continue to drive demands for domestic partner benefits and considerations (for both same-sex and opposite-sex partners and for family members who reside under one roof). The caregiving responsibilities of single parents and of employees who are trying to take care of aged parents or other family members will mean more requests for flexible scheduling and other kinds of workplace considerations. At the same time, the rising cost of benefits and curtailed budgets may mean that library employers will feel they must reduce the number and types of family members eligible for benefits and reduce the flexibility offered to employees.

Planning to Plan

Each of the remaining five chapters in this book addresses a specific human resources topic and project. The five projects are each divided into tasks and steps to provide a framework for completing the projects. While the tasks and steps within each chapter are linear in nature, the five projects in this book do not have to be completed in any particular order. Managers in one library might want to focus on the staffing required to implement the activities in a new strategic plan, in which case they would complete the task and steps in chapter 2. Managers in another library might decide to address the problems it has had with recruitment and would focus on the task and steps in chapter 4. Managers in some libraries might identify several different projects to be carried out at different times, and of course, some managers will complete all of the projects in this book in the order they are presented. The decisions you make will depend on the conditions in your library.

The subjects that HR processes deal with (recruitment, pay, job design and description, organizational structure, staff development, performance evaluation) strike at the very core of our being as employees. It is important, as library managers undertake some or all of the tasks described in this book, to pay attention to how the projects related to those tasks will be planned, managed, and implemented. In some cases, one or two people will be involved in planning and carrying out an HR project. In others, a committee or task force will be appointed to both assist in planning and developing the project and in providing a valuable communications link between the project and the library's employees. Because HR topics are so important and so sensitive, it is likely that you'll want to involve a staff group of some type in most HR projects. Libraries often determine that this group will be a task force, since its existence will be for the term of the project only, not ongoing as a committee usually is.

Each of the projects described in the following chapters will require the same pre-planning. You will need to start by clearly defining the project you plan to undertake in your library. You will then select the people who will be responsible for managing the project and you will write a project committee charge. Finally, you will develop a project communication plan, to ensure that all of the stakeholders are kept informed throughout the project.

Define the Project

A full-blown description of project management tools and techniques is beyond the scope of this book, but a few reminders and references may help you think through the steps of developing your HR project. These steps aren't unique to an HR project; they are general steps for managing any project you might undertake in your library.

One of the best, most practical books on the topic defines project management this way: "Project management is the process by which actions are planned, resources organized, and activities initiated and managed to achieve a specific goal or purpose or to produce a specified deliverable."[7]

This definition basically captures the steps in any project-planning activity:

1. Define the project intent.
2. Identify needed resources and project constraints.
3. Identify potential trouble areas or hot spots.
4. Break the project down into major and minor subdivisions, and identify the tasks that go with each.
5. Sequence the necessary tasks and develop a tracking methodology to be sure you're on track.
6. Assign responsibility for each part of the project.
7. Prioritize and schedule each task.
8. Develop the project budget.
9. Review the plan, revise it as necessary, and obtain final approval.

The first step in the list is also the most important one. Everything else will flow from the definition of the project intent. The project intent is a statement of the purpose for undertaking the HR project. It's important that the definition of the intent of the project be unambiguous and that it include a clear statement of what you expect to accomplish.

If managers in two different libraries decide to initiate projects to review and refine the performance management processes (chapter 5) in their libraries, it is probable that the intent of their projects would be somewhat different. For example, one might write this statement of purpose: "Create a performance management system that is clearly linked to the objectives in the library's strategic plan." Managers in another library might have a different purpose for creating a performance management process: "Create a performance management process that conforms to the newly revised county performance management process." As you can see, the results of the two projects would probably be quite different. However, if the project intent statement for the two projects just said, "Create a performance management process for the library," there would be no reason to assume that the end product would link to the library's strategic plan or conform to the county performance management process.

Select the Project Committee

As noted earlier, because HR projects are so important and so potentially sensitive, it is a good idea to involve staff in the project from the beginning. If you decide to form a committee to work on one or more of the HR projects in this book or to provide advice to a project manager, you'll have to appoint and notify the committee's members. Then you will need to assess their skills and make a preliminary decision about whether or not you will need to involve outside experts in the project. When these decisions are made, you will be able to develop a plan to keep all of the stakeholders informed about the project.

Appointing a project committee is one of the most important tasks in any project. If the committee chair is skilled and committee members are competent and involved, your project is likely to be a success. A committee made up of members who have a history of failing to reach agreement, personal conflicts, and inability to meet deadlines, or members who simply lack the skills needed to find and evaluate information, will almost always result in a failed project.

The project committee should consist of people with the appropriate knowledge to research and make recommendations about HR issues. If your library staff is represented by one or more bargaining units or a staff association, representatives of these organizations should probably be included on the committee. Local conditions and practices will vary, so the decisions about inclusion will be different from library to library. Leadership of the committee should rest with a single person, the committee chair. The committee chair's skills and abilities may be more important than his or her position within the library's organizational structure. The chair must be experienced and skilled in leading groups. The chair should also have a proven track record in project management, including setting and meeting deadlines, collecting and analyzing data, keeping all stakeholders informed, and keeping a project committee on task. It is critical that the chair believe in and support the project being considered.

Committee members might also come from the library's parent jurisdiction, such as a city or county HR department. Library HR analysts or specialists may play a leadership role in the activities of the committee, with library staff members making up the membership of the committee. If your library board has a personnel committee, the relationship between that committee and the project committee should be clarified from the start. The project committee may submit recommendations to the board committee, meet to brief them on the project committee's activities and recommendations, or work with them in some other defined way.

City or county HR analysts might serve as resources to the committee rather than as leaders or members. Outside experts, such as consultants, might also be called upon as resources for the committee to draw upon to do its work. Consultants are often hired to conduct employee climate or satisfaction surveys, for example, both because of their expertise in designing and administering surveys and because they are viewed as neutral outsiders not affiliated with the library administration.

Create the Committee Charge

An effective way to capture the project intent and the responsibility of the project committee is to create a committee charge (some libraries or consultants might use the term *charter*). Such a charge could include the purpose or mission of the committee, the time frame for the project, any parameters that might exist (budget, constraints, resources available), and a list of specific project outcomes or deliverables. The charge should be a document that clearly outlines the expectations that library management has of the committee and the project's intent and scope.

A sample charge, shown in figure 4, was developed for the Tree County Library's Compensation and Classification Study Committee. It can be easily modified for a committee working on any of the HR processes covered in this book. The sample charge provides a comprehensive picture of the project's goals, what is expected of the committee members, the boundaries of the project, the role of the committee members (sounding board, steering or review committee, advocates for the process, communication links to the rest of the staff), the decisions they will make, and the work activities and products they will review. Workform 1, Committee Charge, provides a template which can be used to create a committee charge for your library.

FIGURE 4
Sample Charge

TREE COUNTY LIBRARY

Compensation and Classification Study Committee

Charge

The purposes of the Compensation and Classification Study Committee are

1. to create a mechanism to ensure pay equity within Tree County Library (TCL) now and in the future, including during times of financial cutbacks, position changes, expansion, and work reorganization

2. to become informed about all aspects of the study and to communicate with TCL staff

3. to manage expectations as well as the pace of implementation in a way that meets the needs of the staff and the work of the project

The Compensation and Classification Study Committee functions as a review committee and will provide support and communications that are important in gaining co-operation of Library staff and eventual acceptance of project recommendations. The committee is a sounding board for project activities and findings, and members will ultimately serve as advocates for the implementation of any study recommendations. The committee is created because Library management values the input of employees into compensation and classification issues.

Each committee member is committed to the successful development of these human resource programs and will bring energy, time, enthusiasm, and thoughtful suggestions to each meeting. In addition, each member of the committee represents other employees and will communicate with them regularly to solicit their ideas and keep them informed of the group's progress.

The work of the committee is estimated to take nine months, from the beginning of the project through the submission of recommendations to the Tree County Library Board of Trustees.

It is anticipated that committee members will participate in three to five meetings (several with an outside consultant in attendance) and will focus attention on the following tasks:

Provide input into and understanding about compensation, classification, and related issues currently facing TCL

Serve as a communication link with other Library system employees

Evaluate positions for internal equity

Provide input into and/or review work products that include the following:

- project work plan
- position description questionnaire
- salary survey, including survey participants and benchmark positions
- feedback from interviews with staff members
- compensation philosophy
- preliminary summary of market findings
- appeals
- other related issues
- draft report of findings and recommendations
- implementation plan

Budget issues: The project consultant is paid from the Classification and Compensation Project budget. Substitutes will be obtained for committee members, if needed by their branch. Mileage will be paid for committee members who travel from their home branch to meetings. No other additional costs are anticipated.

Meetings with the project consultant will be scheduled at key project milestones and members will be notified at least two weeks in advance of each meeting date. Committee meetings will last no longer than two hours and will be held in Meeting Room A of TCL headquarters. Committee members will rotate taking action minutes, which will be posted on the project site on the staff intranet, upon approval.

It is expected that members of the committee will keep group discussions and preliminary findings of the consultants confidential until the appropriate time, as determined by the committee and project consultants.

Develop the Communications Plan

No matter how many people are involved in managing the HR project, it's important to think through how information about the project and the progress being made on the project will be communicated. Anything that impacts an employee's work life is potentially sensitive. As the project is being developed, think about who needs to know about it and what form of communication will work best. Hearing through the library grapevine that a succession plan is being developed, for example, could cause employees to think that some of them are being handpicked for future positions, in violation of a union contract or established personnel procedures. They need to be informed about workforce planning and how such planning can take place within a competitive hiring environment. They will want to know how such planning affects them and their colleagues.

The library director, key library managers, the library board, and city and county managers and policy-makers may all be part of the communications process. There may also be times when the media needs to be included in the communications plan. The project manager or committee must be sure that they know when and how to include all of these people and at what part of the project. Will they be personally involved? Will they expect to receive progress reports? Do they make decisions at key junctures or approve final findings and recommendations? Will these decisions be made at a formal meeting, by e-mail or a conference call, or in some other way? A project can run aground if these questions haven't been answered initially, as the project plan is being developed.

There are many guides available for writing communications plans. Plans can be fairly simple or quite elaborate, depending on the project and its complexity and duration. There are key elements to any communications plan that you will want to include:

What. Define the activities, events, and occurrences that are to be communicated. These might include a project kickoff event, a planning meeting, committee meetings, project status reports, major milestone reports, and draft and final reports.

When. Indicate at what points various communications will take place. For example, a report on the kickoff event would be at the beginning of the project, committee meetings might be weekly or monthly, and the final report would be at the end of the project.

How. Not all of your communications will be or should be the same. The kickoff event might be an all-staff meeting. Committee meetings would probably be documented through minutes placed on the staff intranet. The final report could be a printed document as well as an electronic version made available in several locations.

Responsibility. Be sure to indicate who will be responsible for each communication. This is usually the downfall of projects that are not well communicated. Name the person or group responsible for producing or delivering each communication. Identify who needs to see each communication and who has to approve it before it is released.

Audiences. There may be one or more audiences for the communications you produce. Think of the individuals, groups, or entities affected by the project and by the communication. Audiences could include staff members, managers, decision-makers (such as the city manager or mayor), policy-makers (such as the members of a city council or county commission), the library board, unions representing library employees, and the general public. Each message, including its content and form, should be carefully prepared to match the needs and interests of the audience. Staff members impacted by an HR project will need and want a more detailed report than the members of a county commission, for example.

Starting the Human Resources Journey

The remainder of this book focuses on a number of HR projects that can be addressed strategically. As noted earlier, you will pick and choose among them, based on your library's needs. If you are trying to determine the human resources that will be required to accomplish the goals and objectives in your strategic plan, start with chapter 2. That chapter will give you the tools to conduct a gap analysis to identify the human resources you need and those that you have, develop the strategies for dealing with gaps, and implement a plan in response to the gaps. If you want to develop effective job descriptions, chapter 3 will provide you with all of the tools you need. In chapter 4 you will learn how to recruit, test, screen, and select new employees. In chapter 5 you will learn how to develop and implement a performance management system. In chapter 6 you will find a number of tools designed to retain a high-performing workforce.

Once you understand the HR principles described in this chapter and you know how—and why—to appoint a project committee, you are ready to move on to the HR project or projects that make sense in your library. That may mean you start with the information in chapter 4, rather than going through the tasks and steps in chapters 2 and 3. Chapters 2–5 can stand alone or they can be used as a road map to completely overhaul the HR environment in your library. The choice is yours.

Notes

1. Peter F. Drucker, *Management: Tasks, Responsibilities, Practices* (New York: HarperBusiness, 1973), 308.
2. Ibid., 306.
3. An extensive listing of statements comparing management and leadership can be found in Stephen R. Covey, *The 8th Habit: From Effectiveness to Greatness* (New York: Free Press, 2004), 360–64.
4. Diane Mayo and Jeanne Goodrich, *Staffing for Results: A Guide to Working Smarter* (Chicago: American Library Association, 2002).
5. Some of these ideas are adapted from John Sullivan, *Rethinking Strategic HR* (Riverwoods, IL: CCH, 2004).
6. Society for Human Resource Management, *SHRM 2004–2005 Workplace Forecast: A Strategic Outlook* (Alexandria, VA: Society for Human Resource Management, 2004).
7. Jeff Crow, *Applying Project Management in the Workplace* (Portland, OR: Blackbird, 1999), 1–2.

Chapter 2

Create Alignment

MILESTONES

By the time you finish this chapter you will be able to

- review your human resources plan in the context of your strategic service plan
- identify activities required to implement your strategic service plan
- conduct a gap analysis to address current and future staff shortages and surpluses
- develop strategies and tactics for dealing with gaps
- implement a plan in response to the gaps found
- monitor, evaluate, revise

On the surface, the necessity to think deeply about the work that needs to be done in your library may seem like an odd requirement. Of course you know what work needs to be done. It isn't the work that's been a problem . . . it's not having enough people to do it! Library work has traditionally seemed straightforward and is divided by function: circulation, reference, children's, cataloging, and other technical services work. Your library might also provide bookmobile, delivery, and other outreach services to residents of a retirement community, inmates in a jail, or to people who live in remote regions of your service area.

As you think about the work that is done in your library, you probably also think about the work that is done that is necessary but is not "library work." Those who do this work include finance clerks, building maintenance workers, and the administrative assistants who work for the library director (and, if you're lucky, a few other managers in the library). You will undoubtedly also think of the technology work that is now essential in most libraries but that is still less familiar or even confusing to library managers. Network administrators, applications managers, and computer installation and repair personnel are required to maintain library services.

What Is the Work to Be Done?

Just as libraries struggle to make a thirty-year-old building function in the twenty-first century, library employees and managers also struggle with the misalignment between the job skills needed and the job skills that staff already possess. The important point to remember is that human resources management is a means to an end, not an end in itself. Before you can determine whether you have the right people doing the right work at the right time, you need to know what the "right work" is and how you will know that it has been accomplished.

Because of habit and past practice, library managers tend to think about the work that needs to be done and the people they need to do the work in terms of job titles and years of experience. For example, "I need a children's librarian" or "I need a reference librarian with five years' experience" is a common approach to staffing. This approach is no longer sufficient. The fact that someone has held a job with the title "children's librarian" for a period of time tells you nothing about what that person knows or can actually do. You may assume that the person can plan and present preschool story programs, because most children's librarians can do that. However, this children's librarian might have worked in a community in which the focus of youth services was on school-age children, and her primary duty might have been to help teachers develop classroom collections to support the curriculum.

Most public jurisdictions require job descriptions, and the details of writing them are described in the next chapter. Typically, a job description describes the nature of the work to be done as well as its level of complexity, the supervision received or provided, the education and experience required, and the physical requirements of the job. People who work with job descriptions call these requirements "KSAs," short for knowledge, skills, and abilities. Some also add "competencies" to the list.

Figure 5 provides definitions of the terms *knowledge, skills, abilities,* and *competencies.* While these definitions seem fairly straightforward, they can be confusing in application. Don't assume someone has a skill just because she has achieved a certain level of education and experience. It is especially important to resist blurring knowledge and skills when the nature of work is being changed by new technology. Libraries now need graphic artists who know both how to design publications using computers and software programs such as Photoshop and how to design effective websites. They need librarians who are experts at using both print and electronic information resources.

But KSAs are not the work to be done; they are statements of qualifications. The actual work is described by the activities that library employees carry out. Ideally, all the activities performed by library employees will either directly reflect what needs to be done to deliver the service priorities described in the library's strategic plan or will be in support of them. Evaluating the human resources needed to carry out and support the activities in your strategic plan will build an infrastructure of documentation that will support you

---
FIGURE 5
KSAs and Competencies

Knowledge refers to the information and concepts acquired through formal education and job experience. For example: "MLS and five years' experience" or "Knowledge and support of the principles of intellectual freedom."

Skills are the manual and mental capabilities acquired through training and work experience, the application of knowledge gained through education or training and practical experience. For example, "Proficiency in Microsoft Word and Excel" or "Skill in problem analysis and resolution."

Abilities are the natural talents, capacities, and aptitudes possessed by employees. For example, "Ability to communicate effectively with a diverse population" or "Ability to recognize and set priorities, and to plan, coordinate, and organize own work."

A *competency* is "a cluster of related knowledge, skills, and attitudes that affects a major part of one's job (a role or responsibility), that correlates with performance on the job, that can be measured against well-accepted standards, and that can be improved via training and development." For example, "Uses teamwork and project management skills to benefit the library and its users" or "Models self-management."

Source: Scott B. Parry, "The Quest for Competencies," *Training* 33, no. 7 (July 1996): 50.

in carrying out the library's service priorities. The "bricks" of this infrastructure are the activities that you select to support your goals. As defined in this book's introduction, *an activity is a grouping of specific tasks that the library will carry out to achieve its goals and objectives, resulting in an output of things done or services delivered.*

Activities provide an effective framework for determining what work needs to be accomplished and for identifying the staff who can do that work. Instead of simply saying "I need a children's librarian," you should use activities to describe the work that needs to be done to create the results you want and the KSAs to describe what an employee must have in order to do that work.

For example, one of the objectives in the Tree County Library strategic plan was, "Each year, at least 500 children ages 0–5 from Spanish-speaking homes will attend programs presented by library staff." Two staff members were working to identify the staff that would be required to implement this activity. Look at the difference in their recommendations:

1. "We need a children's librarian with at least five years' experience."
2. "We need a children's librarian who speaks Spanish fluently, can present programs to children aged 0–5 and their families, and is able to work with local businesses and organizations to raise funds for our outreach programs."

The first statement simply describes the person's education and years of experience. The second statement focuses on KSAs. The knowledge is the MLS degree and the specialty in children's work, the skill is speaking Spanish fluently and presenting programs, and the ability or competency is working easily with local businesses and organizations. Don't make the mistake of emphasizing the "K" in the KSAs and forgetting to consider the skills and abilities you also need. That is, someone with an MLS degree, a specialty in children's services, and fluency in Spanish would not qualify for this position if she could not easily connect with members of the local business community.

Most library directors and staff members are keenly aware that the work they are doing is changing as the needs and desires of their library customers change and evolve. Virtually every library in the country now provides public computers and access to the Internet, as well as web and electronic resources. Many libraries have noted the work schedules of their residents and have made changes in the times when storytimes and children's programming are offered. Other libraries have responded to their customers' desire for convenience and have made it easier to request and pick up desired materials, apply for a library card, or schedule a meeting room online. Still others have observed that the demographics of their community are changing and that they need books and other materials in languages other than English, as well as materials to meet the needs of newcomers, home-based business owners, English language learners, or young retirees. As a manager, you know that staff with the appropriate KSAs are the key to successfully providing all the services that the library provides or plans to provide.

Your strategic plan spells out what services the library wants to provide during the next several years. These services were defined by assessing the community's needs. The library's challenge is to respond to these needs with the human resources it has now or can acquire. The task and steps in this chapter will guide you through a process to identify the staff KSAs you need to implement your strategic plan.

What If You Don't Have a Plan?

If your library has used the *New Planning for Results* planning process, you know what your library's priorities are, and you can look at how your HR management practices work to support those priorities. If you don't have a strategic plan of service, you can still use the techniques provided in this book. However, you will need to have identified the service goals for your unit, department, or for the library as a whole. Following the practices in this book will help you to identify and develop the staff that are needed to accomplish the library's priorities. *Before you can determine the most effective and efficient staffing configurations for your library, you must know what you expect that staff to accomplish!* This is a key concept that differentiates this book from other, more procedural HR books.

Activity-Based Implementation

It is sometimes hard for staff to see the relationship between the library's strategic plan and the everyday work they do at the library. The activities selected to support the library's goals and objectives should include all of the "real work" (that is, the everyday work) of the staff, as well as activities related to new or enhanced services or programs.

Other identified activities will include the everyday work of support staff (such as finance specialists in the library's office, or delivery drivers) and the work that is performed to develop organizational competencies. An organizational competency is an institutional capacity or efficiency that is necessary to enable the library to achieve the goals and objectives in its strategic plan. For example, a library might find that it isn't collecting all the data elements required by the objectives in its strategic plan. The organizational competency the library would need to develop would be incorporating effective measurements and evaluation into all its operational practices. There would be a number of activities or initiatives that would have to be carried out to develop this competency. All resource allocation, including the strategic HR work we talk about in this book, *should start at the activity level.*

This concept is key to this book and is what links this book to the other books in the Results series. It provides the framework for the HR actions you will undertake because all of your HR actions must be in support of the activities you've selected to implement your strategic plan of service. That is what makes this approach to HR strategic rather than solely tactical.

Identifying Activities

Activities are the actions taken by staff to implement the goals in the library's strategic plan. It is not uncommon for a single activity to support several objectives under a single goal, and some activities support more than one goal in the plan. All activity statements start with an action verb and describe the services to be delivered or the outputs produced.

For example, circulation activities support both of the goals in this statement: "Adults will be able to find high-interest, high-demand materials in a variety of formats to satisfy their interest in current trends and popular culture and to provide enjoyable recreational experiences, and children and teens (ages 5–18) will have services and materials in a variety of formats that stimulate their imaginations and provide enjoyable recreational experiences." Other activities are carried out to support those who perform these activities (business office and IT support work) or to develop an organizational competency, as was explained earlier in this chapter.

How do you transition from broad service goals to daily and yearly activities for each library employee? You may have already identified activities as part of your planning process. If you haven't, here's a description of how to do it. Using this process to involve staff in selecting activities will make this transitional process real and relevant to them.

1. Distribute the goals and objectives you've developed through your planning process to the work units and branches (if your library has branches) in your library.
2. Set up meetings for staff in work units or branches to come together to talk about the work they are currently doing that relates to each goal in the plan. Ask each staff member to develop a list of their current activities that support each goal in the plan. A "current activity" is an activity you plan to provide exactly as it is being provided now. The activity will require no new resources, and you do not plan to reduce the resources currently allocated to support it.
3. Ask a staff member to read his or her first activity, and record it on a flip chart. Ask if anyone else identified a similar activity. If so, merge the activities into

a single activity before recording it. Work with the group to be sure that the activities they identified are not really tasks or steps (see definitions provided in the introduction). If they are, remove them from the list.

4. Continue to record, merge, and confirm that identified activities really are activities until all the staff members involved have had a chance to talk about all the activities they have identified.

5. Next, identify activities that are modified or new. A modified activity is an activity that you are currently providing and plan to continue to offer in a modified form. You may be planning to expand the activity by adding more resources to support it; you may be planning to limit the activity by reducing the resources allocated to support it; or you may decide to do it differently. A new activity is an activity that is not being offered in any form in your library at this time. Depending on the size of the work group and the time available, you may want to identify modified and new activities during a second meeting.

6. Review the plan's goals and objectives again (especially important if this is a second meeting) and ask the group to brainstorm modified and new activities that would support the goals of the plan. Give the members of the group a few minutes to think about these activities (provide them with the definitions of each).

7. Ask each staff member to provide one idea for a new or modified activity. Record the idea on a flip chart and move on to the next staff member. Continue until all have had a chance to state their ideas. Work through each goal in the plan, asking for ideas from each staff member.

8. Review the recorded activities, merging similar activities and deleting steps and tasks, as was done with current activities above.

9. Using the listing of current, modified, and new activities, review with the group members the process for evaluating the effectiveness of each activity in relation to the goals and objectives of the plan. Ask them to rank each activity using the effectiveness scale in figure 6. Explain that their suggestions and the same sort of ranking process will be used to make the final determination of the activities that will ultimately be selected to implement the library's plan.

Activities can represent a global or broad view of library services or a local or more specific view. Normally lists of activities generated by staff will include both points of view. Library managers will have to find a middle ground between global and local activities when they make the final selection. Figure 7 provides an example of each point of view.

After library management has selected the activities to be carried out, be sure to let employees know which of the many activities suggested have been selected. Be sure to emphasize to them how their work either is one or more of the activities selected or contributes to or supports the activities selected. You will also want to provide a list of the activities that will be reduced or eliminated, either because they do not support any of the goals in the library's strategic plan or because they were determined to be less effective than others during the activity evaluation and review process. This is a critical part of this process. Otherwise staff are likely to think they will be expected to do everything they are currently doing *plus* all of the new or enhanced activities that have been selected.

FIGURE 6
Evaluating Effectiveness

The *effectiveness* of an activity is a measure of the potential of that activity to contribute to producing an identified result.

Effectiveness can be measured by three elements, each of which has a five-level scale:

Effectiveness Scale

Target Audience	Result Produced	Audience Response
1 = 40% of the audience	1 = Very high	1 = Users will love it
2 = 25% of the audience	2 = High	2 = Users will like it a lot
3 = 10% of the audience	3 = Moderate	3 = Users will think it is OK
4 = 5% of the audience	4 = Low	4 = Users will not care much
5 = 1% or less of the audience	5 = None	5 = Users will not care at all

Target Audience

Percentage of Audience Served: The target audience for most activities is defined demographically (usually by age) or by condition (illiterate, new parent, etc.). The *potential* target audience for most activities should be all people who fit within the demographic or condition profile. This is a measure of the percentage of the total potential audience who will be reached by the activity at least once. Programs that serve the same people repeatedly are less effective than those in which the audience varies.

Delivery Time and Place: Programs designed to serve specific target audiences may be less effective because they are not delivered at times or in places appropriate for those audiences. As a result they will reach fewer members of the target audience and receive a lower ranking.

If an activity ranks 4 or 5 on the *Target Audience* scale, it is not effective. No further evaluation is necessary. If an activity ranks 1, 2, or 3, evaluate the *Result Produced*.

Result Produced

Services: The services provided by the activity must contribute to producing a result identified in one or more objectives for the goal this activity addresses. This is a measure of the degree to which an activity will contribute to meeting the measure of progress in one or more objectives. Activities that contribute to more than one objective for the goal produce greater results than those that just contribute to one objective.

If an activity ranks 4 or 5 on the *Result Produced* scale, it is not effective. No further evaluation is necessary. If an activity ranks 1, 2, or 3, evaluate the *Audience Response*.

Audience Response

Emotional Response: This is the most intangible of the three elements. Effective activities appeal to the intended users. The more appealing the activities are, the more likely they are to be effective. This measure is only used to evaluate activities that have already been determined to serve the target audience and contribute to producing the desired results.

FIGURE 7
Activity Views

Global/Broad View	Local/Narrow View	Middle Ground
Provide public programming for adults	Present computer programs for seniors in the library	Provide stand-alone adult programming events in the library
	Present computer programs for seniors in Senior Centers	Provide series of adult programs intended for the same audience in the library
	Present computer programs in the library for Spanish-speaking immigrants	Provide adult programming in off-site location
	Lead monthly book club	Cosponsor adult programs with local agencies
	Design and present a series of programs on local history	
	Collaborate with the County Extension Service to provide programs for new parents	

Communicating this process throughout the library will show how goals, objectives, and activities flow up from the individual employee level to enable your library to accomplish its priorities. Depending on the size of your library, you may also want to aggregate activities at the department or work unit level. However, remember that many of the activities will cross department lines. You don't want the approach you take to grouping activities to compartmentalize them. Instead, use the process to break down or soften work unit, department, or facility-to-facility barriers and to promote the concept of library employees working together as a team to implement the library's strategic goals.

Individual employees carry out the activities identified. Each employee needs to know what she is supposed to do, how well she is supposed to do it (chapter 5 will discuss performance planning and evaluation), and how her duties and responsibilities fit into the big picture of the library.

Gap Analysis

This chapter focuses on examining the type, number, and KSAs of staff you need to accomplish the activities that support your goals; determining what staff resources you have that are currently allocated to support those activities; comparing them to see the gap between the two; and finally developing a plan to address that gap. This process is called *gap analysis* and was first introduced in the original *Planning for Results* book.

Gap analysis is not just used to assess the human resources needed to implement the activities in your strategic plan. It is also used to identify the technology infrastructure that will be required (see *Technology for Results: Developing Service-Based Plans*), the facility resources that will be required (see *Managing Facilities for Results: Optimizing Space for Services*), and the materials collection that will be required (see the third chapter in *Managing for Results: Effective Resource Allocation for Public Libraries*). If you have worked with the gap analysis process before, you will find it easy to complete the steps in this task. If this is your introduction to gap analysis, the steps in this task and the accompanying workform will provide you with all the guidance you need to understand and use the process effectively to determine the staffing resources you need.

Workform 2, Gap Analysis, provides a structured way to determine the staff you need to carry out an identified activity, the staff you have already assigned to that activity, and the difference between the two (the gap or the surplus). The staffing plan you come up with after conducting this analysis will specify how you will bridge the gap: reallocate staff hours from other, lower-priority activities; provide needed training and skills development to equip current staff with the knowledge, skills, and abilities needed to implement the activity; or (this will be the rarer case) hire additional staff with the needed KSAs.

Will you have to perform gap analysis on every activity you select? Definitely not. You can use this tool to determine what staff resources you'll need to undertake activities that are new to your library or much expanded beyond the current level. You might also want to use the tool as a way to determine what you do need for ongoing activities or to see which staff resources could be redeployed. One way to determine whether or not you need to perform a gap analysis would be to ask yourself: Can we do this? If you and your staff think you can without difficulty, the analysis probably isn't necessary. However, if you find yourself wondering how in the world you'll be able to undertake the new activity as well as all the other activities you perform, you should definitely perform a gap analysis to figure out what you will need in terms of KSAs and staff time.

This is all about making tough choices. Selecting activities requires evaluation and winnowing. Remind yourself, other staff members, and your library board that you can't do it all. Some activities, including ones that are or have been highly valued, will by necessity need to be eliminated. This process requires you to consider, through the identification of current, modified, and new activities, what you will continue doing or will do less of, as well as what you will take on that is new. Since most library employees feel that they are fully utilized already, there is no way to take on new activities unless some of the current ones are eliminated or reduced.

Workforce Planning and Gap Analysis

Faced with a large number of impending retirements and fewer graduates in essential disciplines, public and private employers are mounting formal and informal efforts to assess and plan their staffing more proactively. Formal processes are normally called workforce planning. "Workforce planning is getting the right number of people with the right set of competencies in the right jobs at the right time."[1] If your city or county has decided to undergo a formal workforce planning program, you could be asked to analyze your staffing needs for the next five to ten years, project what types and numbers of staff you might realistically have available (taking attrition rates into account) at any given time, identify the external factors that will affect your staffing, and thoroughly review what your work will be and how you will do it. This form of workforce planning is broader and more global than what is being proposed in this book.

Now that you have identified the activities that will be included in your plan, you are ready to start assessing the staff resources that will be required to implement those activities.

TASK 1: ASSESS REQUIRED STAFF RESOURCES

Task 1: Assess Required Staff Resources
    Step 1.1: Plan the project
    Step 1.2: Determine what you need
    Step 1.3: Determine what you have
    Step 1.4: Identify the gap
    Step 1.5: Develop a plan to bridge the gap
    Step 1.6: Implement the plan
Task 2: Describe the Job
Task 3: Identify the Right Person for the Right Job
Task 4: Develop and Implement a Performance
        Management System
Task 5: Develop and Implement a Retention Plan

Step 1.1
Plan the Project

If you are going to complete this task, refer back to the "Planning to Plan" section of chapter 1. This information will help you plan the project, determine whether you need a committee and, if so, select committee members, create a charge, and formulate a communications plan.

Step 1.2
Determine What You Need

It is very difficult for most people to look at a three-year strategic plan for a library and identify the human resources that will be needed to implement that plan. The view is so global that it is hard to find the forest, let alone the trees within the forest. For example, the Tree County Public Library strategic plan included this goal: "K–8 students in Tree County will have access to materials, programs, and services that will help them succeed in school." Can you list the human resources requirements to meet this goal? As you start to try to answer that question, you will probably find yourself saying, "What would we do to make this happen?" In other words, you would start to identify activities.

There are hundreds of activities that you might select that could support this broad goal. The only way to select from among those activities is to have a clear picture of how you are going to measure your progress toward reaching the goal. The Tree County Public Library used the *Planning for Results* process, so the objectives in the plan described how progress would be measured. One of the objectives for this goal was: "By FY 2XXX, the visits to Tree County Library homework web pages will increase from 100,000 (the FY 2XXX level) to 150,000." This is considerably more specific than the goal. Can you list the HR requirements for this objective? Again, you will probably find yourself asking, "What would we have to do to make this happen?" And so we are right back to activities.

Activities in support of this objective could include finding out what the local school curricula are for grades K–8; identifying the library and community resources required to support these curricula; designing, developing, and determining how to maintain a homework assistance web page; identifying special educational initiatives in Tree County; and so on. Now you are at the point of describing some HR needs:

- Someone who knows how to contact county schools and acquire curriculum guides

- Someone who knows how to collaborate effectively with local schools
- Someone who can select the appropriate support materials for the library collection
- Someone who can design, develop, and create a means for maintaining the library's homework assistance web page
- Someone who can assess electronic resources that should be linked to the homework assistance web page
- Someone who can assess whether or not the web page is meeting user needs and can then make (or seek help in making) needed improvements to it

Note that all of these needs are expressed in terms of KSAs: someone who knows how to; someone who can (i.e., has the skills to); someone to make contacts (i.e., has the ability to).

In addition to determining the KSAs required by an activity, you will also need to estimate how many hours a week or fractions of a full-time equivalent (FTE) will be needed to carry out the activity. If the activity represents everyday activities such as checking books in and out, searching for holds, or answering customers' questions, you probably have a pretty good idea what you need.

If the activity is a new one, you will have to estimate the amount of time or number of FTEs you think will be required to carry it out. You may have done this sort of thing when preparing a grant or project proposal. The hours or FTEs needed will either be a best guess or estimate based on past experience or they may be what you can allocate, which means the activity will have to be shaped to be carried out within the number of hours allocated to it.

Figure 8 shows what Workform 2 would look like with this information entered into it. You may notice that figure 8 lists only one knowledge, one skill, and one ability. That is because those KSAs are the most important elements for this particular activity. When completing a gap analysis for a more complex activity, you may well have more than one knowledge, skill, and ability.

FIGURE 8
Gap Analysis Example—Need

WORKFORM 2   **Gap Analysis**

B. Staff resource required to accomplish activity:	C. Need
XX hours or FTEs of library staff time to plan and develop K–8 homework assistance web page	Knowledge: Someone who knows how to find and utilize library resources in support of K–8 homework assistance
	Skills: Someone who knows how to design, develop, and maintain a website
	Abilities: Someone who can make contacts with local schools, obtain curricula for grades K–8, develop and foster a collaborative relationship with teachers and administrators
	Hours or FTE: XX hours estimated for this activity

The identified activities will ultimately be assigned to a staff member (or members) and will become part of her (or their) performance management plan (see chapter 5).

Step 1.3
Determine What You Have

For ongoing activities, you may think you know what you have. You can look at your budget to see how many hours or FTEs have been allocated to some activities, but the breakdown is probably not as detailed as you need for many activities. You might have 2.5 FTE children's librarians budgeted, but this tells you nothing about the knowledge, skills, and abilities of these children's librarians. If your activity is to provide services to Spanish-speaking families in your community, for example, you will have to dig deeper. Just looking at FTEs or hours won't provide you with the complete picture of what you have.

When evaluating what KSAs you have on staff, don't forget that over the last decade, public library managers and staff members have become familiar with subject areas that were previously less known to them. Look for knowledge and skills such as child development, multicultural programming, marketing, merchandising, community analysis, web design and usability testing, foreign book trade practices, facilities planning and maintenance, technology planning and implementation, public finance and budgeting, communications and public relations, adult learning and training, fund-raising, community collaboration, public policy development, and project management. The typical library manager or employee with twenty to thirty years' experience has had to gain required knowledge and experience in these areas on the job and on the fly.

The Tree County Library, for example, discovered that one of its newly hired reference librarians had had an earlier career in web development. She was new to librarianship, but she brought a wealth of experience in just the kind of web design and development that the library needed to pursue as activities in developing an effective homework assistance website.

Figure 9 shows an example of the "Have" section of Workform 2 filled out.

Knowing what you have is more than just identifying positions, KSAs, and the number of staff or hours available. It will also involve identifying possibilities for reallocating staff. To do this you'll need to know how staff are currently spending their time. Most library staff members are not sitting around with extra time on their hands. *Staffing for Results: A Guide to Working Smarter,* an earlier book in the Results series, provides the methodology and workforms to help you determine what work is currently being done by staff and how it is being done. Two methods for analyzing work are explained: *numeric analysis,* which measures the amount of work being accomplished by the staff you have, and *process analysis,* which identifies the actual steps and tasks that it takes to produce the work that is being done.

Libraries using the techniques provided in *Staffing for Results* have been able to reallocate staff to the activities they've identified as most effective for implementing their strategic plans. For example, numeric analysis can provide the answer to the question: How long does it take to prepare for a bilingual storytime? A library can then reallocate staff to this activity, find volunteers to assist with the activity if time can't be taken away from other activities, or find ways to eliminate or change how other activities are done. Process analysis provides the information needed to change how the activity is done by reducing

FIGURE 9

Gap Analysis Example—Have

WORKFORM 2   **Gap Analysis**

B. Staff resource required to accomplish activity: XX hours or FTEs of library staff time to plan and develop K–8 homework assistance web page	C. Need	D. Have
	Knowledge: Someone who knows how to find and utilize library resources in support of K–8 homework assistance	Knowledge: Two children's librarians with extensive knowledge of library collections; limited knowledge of specific K–8 curricula; familiarity with local schools through school visits
	Skills: Someone who knows how to design, develop, and maintain a website	Skills: Reference librarian who has experience from previous job in developing, designing, and maintaining website
	Abilities: Someone who can make contacts with local schools, obtain curricula for grades K–8, develop and foster a collaborative relationship with teachers and administrators	Abilities: Branch manager who has had experience working with community agencies, including local schools; enjoys developing community contacts and partnerships
	Hours or FTE: XX hours estimated for this activity	Hours or FTE: X hours available: most hours scheduled on public service desks, some community work already being done

or eliminating the steps in a task or the tasks of an activity. It answers the questions: What are the steps involved in preparing for a bilingual storytime? How long does each step take? Taken together, numeric and process analyses provide much-needed information that can be used to reassign staff hours to higher-priority activities.

Step 1.4
Identify the Gap

Gap analysis involves comparing what you need to carry out an activity with the staff you have to carry out that activity. This comparison will result in the identification of both gaps (projected supply doesn't match up with forecast need or demand) and surpluses (more supply than need or demand). The gaps or surpluses might be in identified KSAs or hours/FTEs or a combination of the two.

As you do your analysis, you may find several types of possible gaps. These could include the following.

1. You have too many staff performing obsolete or declining activities or ones likely to be outsourced. Years ago, library technical services departments had cadres of typists and file clerks. All of that work is gone now, although the functions of preparing catalog records and making them available to library users still exist in a different format. Will

you need as many circulation clerks after you've installed self-checkout machines? As library customers continue to use the Internet to find factual information, will you need as many reference librarians? Will you be replacing MLS-degreed librarians with para-professionals, as you determine that many of the questions asked at public service desks are actually informational or directional rather than higher-level reference or research questions? Because most staff feel they have too much to do already, it will be difficult to think that you might have "too many" staff doing some things, but your gap analysis and the *Staffing for Results* analyses mentioned earlier in this chapter could uncover opportunities to reassign or reallocate staff to the activities that are now top priorities.

2. You currently do not have enough people in the job titles and position descriptions that will remain basically the same as they are now. In other words, you will need more people doing work that you currently have and you've determined that this work won't really change that much in the future. With patron-placed holds, for example, you might find that you will need as many if not more pages, circulation clerks, and delivery staff to handle the large number of materials moving among facilities. If your strategic plan calls for activities that promote increased circulation, you may find gaps between what you need and the staff you now have in these positions.

3. You do not have enough people with the skill sets and competencies that you have determined will be needed in the future. You may see that you need more people who can conduct effective outreach with people who speak languages other than English or who are from different cultures, or more people who can develop and manage projects. Again, your analysis of needed KSAs and competencies will drive your gap analysis conclusions.

Figure 10 provides an example of Workform 2 filled out showing the gaps that have been identified.

Step 1.5
Develop a Plan to Bridge the Gap

The last section of Workform 2 asks for your plan to fill the gap or reallocate the surplus. This step provides you with ways to determine how to do that for each gap analysis you perform. Remember, you don't have to perform a gap analysis for all activities, only those with significant staffing implications.

As was explained in chapter 1, strategies refer to broad approaches to achieving a goal, while tactics are short-term or smaller-scale actions. You will have to develop both tactics and strategies as you determine solutions to your identified staffing needs.

Develop Strategies and Tactics

There are a number of strategies and tactics you can consider to address future gaps and surpluses. The ones you choose will depend on a number of factors:

The amount of time you have. Do you have enough time to develop staff internally? Do you need critical KSAs and competencies right now? Can you conduct a fast, effective recruitment to obtain the needed KSAs and competencies?

The resources you already have. Do staff members have the KSAs and competencies required or the potential and desire to develop them? Do you have the resources necessary to develop job descriptions and recruit, test, select, and train new employees? Is your compensation such that you will be able to attract people with the characteristics you need?

FIGURE 10

Gap Analysis Example—Gap

WORKFORM 2 **Gap Analysis**

B. Staff resource required to accomplish activity:	C. Need	D. Have	E. Gap/Surplus
XX hours or FTEs of library staff time to plan and develop K–8 homework assistance web page	Knowledge: Someone who knows how to find and utilize library resources in support of K–8 homework assistance Skills: Someone who knows how to design, develop, and maintain a website Abilities: Someone who can make contacts with local schools, obtain curricula for grades K–8, develop and foster a collaborative relationship with teachers and administrators Hours or FTE: XX hours estimated for this activity	Knowledge: Two children's librarians with extensive knowledge of library collections; limited knowledge of specific K–8 curricula; familiarity with local schools through school visits Skills: Reference librarian who has experience from previous job in developing, designing, and maintaining website Abilities: Branch manager who has had experience working with community agencies, including local schools; enjoys developing community contacts and partnerships Hours or FTE: X hours available: most hours scheduled on public service desks, some community work already being done	Knowledge: Need specific knowledge of K–8 curricula Skills: Need to broaden web design, development, and maintenance skills; can't rely upon just one person Abilities: Children's librarians need coaching to become more confident in making school and community contacts Hours or FTE: XX hours required to design, develop, and maintain web page; XX hours required to establish and maintain contacts with schools

Your internal depth. Gauging internal depth or "bench strength" is another way of looking at the personnel resources you have. Do staff members already working for you have the potential and interest to take on new or modified positions, or will it be necessary to go outside to find what you need? Are there staff in the "pipeline" developing the talent and skills you will need? Are you working to develop the pipeline?

Your competition. The local competition you have for "in-demand" skills and competencies needs to be considered. Will you be competing with other employers for the same skills? Do you remember the frantic Y2K preparations to ensure that computers could handle the date rollover from 1999 to 2000? During that time, libraries found it very difficult to hire qualified information-technology support people and network analysts. A couple of years later, a number of IT professionals, laid off after the dot-com bust, were looking for work. If you find that the hot skills you need are also in heavy demand by others in your hiring market, you might conclude that it makes more sense to develop internal staff members to take on the jobs that will be created or even to outsource the work or retain someone on a contractual basis.

Workplace and workforce dynamics. Workplace and workforce dynamics will also play a major role in influencing the strategies that you choose to deploy. Do you have the flexibility to move employees if workload or productivity declines? Are there union contracts, personnel policies, or work rules that must be considered and possibly rewritten or renegotiated? Have you adopted streamlined or automated techniques that have changed the nature of the work that is done or how it is done? Have you written flexible job descriptions? Have you cross-trained to allow employees to be moved among different units fluidly in response to changing customer or staffing needs?

Compensation and job classifications. Current job classifications, position descriptions, and compensation plans may not reflect or reward the future functional requirements and competencies needed by the library. Does the structure of the classification system (for example, a job series such as Librarian I, II, III) have enough flexibility to recognize competency growth and employee succession in a timely fashion? Alternatively, are the differences in the levels representative of additional competencies and skills that add value, or are they based on "seat time" only? Are job descriptions written so narrowly that clerks balk at mailing out borrowers' cards because their job description doesn't mention mailing things? Does the compensation plan allow for flexibility in compensation? The tools and techniques in *Developing a Compensation Plan for Your Library* will help you think through, modify, and update your compensation and classification plans if this is needed to reflect and reward new realities.[2]

Figure 11 is a table of some of the challenges discussed in this section and the strategies and tactics that might work to solve them. Many of these will be discussed at greater length throughout the balance of this book.

Figure 12 shows Workform 2 fully completed. Remember that this form is completed for the staff required by an activity.

Before the individual activity staffing plan can be implemented, the appropriate review and approval steps must be taken. These will vary from library to library, but it's important to remember that the director and possibly the library board need to review and sign off before the implementation of the plan can begin.

FIGURE 11
Challenges, Strategies, and Tactics

Challenge (Gap/Surplus)	Strategy	Tactics
Position classifications don't meet current or future needs	Create position classifications that will • support the library's strategic plan • help find, keep, and deploy the right people doing the right things at the right time and in the right place	• Review classification titles and descriptions • Develop a broader classification series • Redefine or consolidate titles; develop new titles • Write competency-based job descriptions and/or position profiles
Compensation offerings	Develop a compensation philosophy, strategy, and system that will attract, promote, and retain employees with the skills and competencies needed	• Study broad compensation bands used in other industries for management and exempt employees • Consider flexible placement within ranges for non-management employees • Consider using incentives and differentials for evening and weekend work • Consider whether your compensation system is motivating or ineffective • Review the benefits, perquisites, and allowances you provide • Consider the intangibles you can offer such as a good work environment or strong quality of life in your community
Succession planning	Address future needs by including "developing a bench"	• Develop specifically designed career paths so that staff will be competitive as jobs open up • Identify probable openings in all key positions where you may not have much depth (interlibrary loan and cataloging are specialty areas in which the knowledge base is unique and often held by only one or a few employees)
Recruitment	Plan to hire the KSAs and competencies needed. Don't be intimidated by a tight labor market or one where hot skills are in demand.	• Target prospective candidates • Think creatively about how you will find and attract the best candidates for your positions • Revise your examination processes so that they encourage rather than discourage candidates

FIGURE 11
Challenges, Strategies, and Tactics (Cont.)

Challenge (Gap/Surplus)	Strategy	Tactics
Training and retraining	Plan training to keep abreast of how quickly library work, work processes, and technology are changing	• Train employees in a variety of modes and pacing • Offer new employee orientation, just-in-time training to update skills, structured curricula, and sequenced training • Provide employees with the opportunity to expand and update their knowledge and skills • Train to assure that identified key competencies are available within the library workforce
Retention	Keep the employees in whom you've invested time and energy to recruit and train	• Evaluate the work environment you provide • Think of ways that you can meet employee needs for time off and flexible schedules • Conduct periodic employee surveys so you know what they are thinking and what motivates them • Think through what it will take to be the employer of choice for your employees
Redeployment, career counseling, transition counseling, separation	Be prepared to help employees deal with the realities of changing needs and services at the library. Be compassionate and professional.	• When employees are redeployed to different work units, facilities, or specialty areas, offer transition and separation counseling • When career paths shorten or close down try to offer other paths • Allow voluntary transfer or demotion • Offer career counseling and transition assistance when employees find that the work they want to do and the work that the library needs done no longer match • Involve the bargaining unit in planning responses to changes
Knowledge transfer	Capture the knowledge of experienced staff members before they leave the library, particularly if they are in unique, one-of-a-kind positions	• Build in a process and enough time so that key documents, manuals, procedures, etc., can be constructed or updated • Consider a mentoring period so that knowledge and experience can be passed along

FIGURE 12
Gap Analysis Example

A. Activity: Analyze Community Demographics

B. Staff resource required to accomplish activity:	C. Need	D. Have	E. Gap/Surplus
XX hours or FTEs of library staff time to plan and develop K–8 homework assistance web page	Knowledge: Someone who knows how to find and utilize library resources in support of K–8 homework assistance Skills: Someone who knows how to design, develop, and maintain a website Abilities: Someone who can make contacts with local schools, obtain curricula for grades K–8, develop and foster a collaborative relationship with teachers and administrators Hours or FTE: XX hours estimated for this activity	Knowledge: Two children's librarians with extensive knowledge of library collections; limited knowledge of specific K–8 curricula; familiarity with local schools through school visits Skills: Reference librarian who has experience from previous job in developing, designing, and maintaining website Abilities: Branch manager who has had experience working with community agencies, including local schools; enjoys developing community contacts and partnerships Hours or FTE: X hours available: most hours scheduled on public service desks, some community work already being done	Knowledge: Need specific knowledge of K–8 curricula Skills: Need to broaden web design, development, and maintenance skills; can't rely upon just one person Abilities: Children's librarians need coaching to become more confident in making school and community contacts Hours or FTE: XX hours required to design, develop, and maintain web page; XX hours required to establish and maintain contacts with schools

F. Plan for filling the gap or relocating the surplus:

Analyze current workload and work processes of children's and reference librarians. Provide coaching by branch manager to children's librarians to increase their confidence and skills in making school and community contacts needed to develop collaborative ways to provide homework assistance through library web page. Determine amount of time that will be needed on ongoing basis to refresh and maintain web page. Provide training for additional staff members so that there is a cadre of staff with web page design, development, and maintenance skills.

Completed by _____

Source of data _____

Date completed _____

Library _____

Step 1.6
Implement the Plan

The planning for implementation should occur at the beginning of the gap analysis process, when you obtain buy-in from your library board, library director, and management team. To achieve complete success, information about the process and the reasons for it should also be communicated to library employees, decision-makers (such as your city council, county commission, and library board), and to other interested parties (such as the union that represents library employees, or a staff association). No one should be surprised that such planning is going on.

Workforce planning is quite common in the public sector. However, looking critically at employees' jobs can make employees very nervous. It's vital that the gap analysis and your planning process be as transparent as possible. Remember to link gap analysis back to what you intend to achieve, the activities that are essential to implementing your plan. You may not feel you can share everything, but you do need to consider what information you can share and what you cannot and why, so that you are prepared to respond in a consistent manner to questions that might come up.

To ensure that your staffing plan is a vital, living document and not just one more thing that takes up shelf space, you must be sure that you relate your staffing plan to your strategic plan and other key activities (such as budget planning and preparation) and documents. You will want to consider how you will include employees in the implementation process, and the unions or employee associations that represent them. You will also want to decide how you will implement the strategies and tactics you selected as you developed the staffing plan. For example, if you decide a tactic is to write new job descriptions, how will you make that happen when you need it to happen?

Depending on your library's structure, you may have to align your library staffing plan with other workforce planning activities that are going on in your parent jurisdiction. You may be part of a larger workforce planning effort and have to make sure that the approach you are taking is congruent with that of the other departments or divisions in your jurisdiction. Or you may find yourself undertaking a more complicated process that involves persuading human resources personnel or others in the parent jurisdiction that the library's staffing planning process is worthwhile and that their assistance in providing data or helping write new job descriptions is a valuable use of time and resources.

Monitor, Evaluate, Revise

This is vital to the success of the plan. You need to check your progress periodically against the time line you've established. Are you progressing as you thought you would, or have some things come up that have slowed down your progress? Have internal or external events created changes that require you to make adjustments to your staffing plan? You will also want to make adjustments as you receive feedback on the plan.

As has been noted in previous books in the Results series, planning is a continuous process. As soon as one planning cycle is completed, it's time to begin the next one. *The New Planning for Results* describes the cycle as having these components: estimate, implement, check, and adjust.[3] *Staffing for Results* explained the process by describing the phases of the plan-do-check-act cycle (sometimes referred to as the Shewhart Cycle or the Deming Cycle).[4] Regardless of the terminology employed, the point is the same: planning must continue and it must be evaluated. As soon as your plan is in place, it has already begun to grow old. Circumstances, the environment in which your library operates, the demographics of your community, and the budget and other resources you have will have changed. These changes, along with what you learn from monitoring the implementation of your plan and listening to the feedback you receive, should all cause you to make adjustments and modifications. At the same time, you will be propelled into the next planning cycle, as you address new workforce and organizational issues that might occur.

This chapter establishes the importance of identifying activities as the foundation of implementing your strategic plan. In chapter 3 you will learn how to incorporate activities into job descriptions, and later, in chapter 5, into employee performance plans.

Notes

1. State of Washington, Department of Personnel, *Workforce Planning Guide: Right People, Right Jobs, Right Time,* December 2000. http://hr.dop.wa.gov/workforceplanning/wfpguide.htm.
2. Paula Singer, *Designing a Compensation Plan for Your Library* (Chicago: American Library Association, 2002).
3. Sandra Nelson, *The New Planning for Results: A Streamlined Approach* (Chicago: American Library Association, 2001), 142.
4. Diane Mayo and Jeanne Goodrich, *Staffing for Results: A Guide to Working Smarter* (Chicago: American Library Association, 2002), 108–9.

Chapter 3

Describe the Job

MILESTONES

By the time you finish this chapter you will be able to

- create and use a position description questionnaire
- analyze jobs
- develop job descriptions

The traditional terminology and approach to staffing (sourcing, recruiting, and hiring employees) reinforced the idea that library employees are as interchangeable as technical services' processing supplies. Many libraries "requisition" or "order" employees. This mind-set represents an outdated notion and reflects a tactical rather than a strategic approach to staffing. The focus is on the immediate details of finding a warm body to fill a vacant "slot" rather than on looking at the big picture of a longer time frame and keying in on meeting the library's needs and goals.

If you're taking the same approach to staffing that you took 20, 10, or even 5 years ago, you're making a big mistake. A bad hiring decision, particularly one that isn't remedied during the probationary period, can haunt you for years, even decades. We often see problem employees or employees who don't have the required technical or interpersonal skills moved from location to location or work unit to work unit in an effort to farm out the unfortunate hiring choice. This practice carries a heavy price in terms of time, energy, and morale.

Staffing needs in libraries today go beyond technical skills and competencies. Even routine jobs require skills and competencies greater than those once required. Years ago, batteries of clerk-typists typed and filed catalog cards, overdue notices, and book order slips. In most public libraries these very routine jobs, with their prescribed tasks and easily described performance standards, are gone. In many libraries, in fact, job titles and job descriptions for low-level clerical positions have been eliminated because jobs of this type no longer exist. Technology is both driving and providing the basis for these shifts. Automated circulation systems prepare and deliver (often via e-mail or automated telephone calls) overdue notices and bills, self-checkout equipment reduces the number of clerks required to assist people, automated equipment tracks and checks in library materials, and online catalogs eliminate the need for typed and filed catalog cards. Technology can reduce the amount of routine work that employees have to do, but it can also increase the experience, skills, and education required of a new employee, as well as the training time that new employee will need.

The work done in libraries and the mix of duties have changed. In a library with well-utilized self-checkout units, circulation clerks who interact with library customers deal with educating them and with resolving problems, because transactions that don't involve problems (such as excessive fines or overdue materials) move easily through the machines. Technology now touches virtually all employees. Pages, delivery drivers, maintenance personnel, shipment packers—in most libraries these positions routinely use the integrated library system, e-mail, and computers. In small libraries, employees must often be masters of a number of tasks. One person is often called upon to perform a number of functions using a variety of technologies, from setting up the circulation desk to researching and answering reference questions, to selecting and ordering library materials.

At the same time, many library organization structures have flattened, either in response to changes in management responsibility, such as the desire to push decision-making down into the organization and improve processes by involving those actually doing the work, or in response to budget cutbacks. As a result, employees are asked not to just show up for work but to actively engage in developing and maintaining high standards of work and customer service. With fewer layers of management, employees are also expected to self-manage. While this is exciting and desirable for many, it is not for those who want or need close supervision or who resent being asked to be the source of ideas and improvements in how things are done.

All of these changes mean that you have to think strategically as you consider the approach you want to take to staffing. Figure 13 represents the differences between the traditional approach to staffing and the new strategic staffing model.

You will want to take great care in defining the knowledge, skills, and abilities (KSAs, defined in figure 5) required to carry out your library's activities and to think clearly and realistically about the jobs you have or need to fill in your library. What will you be expecting an employee to accomplish? What skills and abilities, in addition to formal education and experience, will be required for her to successfully achieve these accomplishments? How will you know whether or not the experience a person has is relevant to what you need her to do? If you performed a gap analysis in chapter 2, you have many if not most of the answers to these questions.

If you didn't conduct a gap analysis, ask yourself what desired results and accomplishments you need. This will help you, as you develop job descriptions, to move beyond what employees may currently be doing in a job to what you will now require of them. If you're developing a job description for a new job, this question will help you crystallize your thinking and help you avoid jumping to conclusions about the skills and abilities that may relate to education and experience.

This chapter will help you write job descriptions that describe the jobs you need performed in your library in order to carry out the activities necessary to provide the services your community wants and needs.

FIGURE 13
Old and New Staffing Models

Old Staffing Paradigm	Strategic Staffing Model
Think "job"	Think tasks and responsibilities that are keyed to the activities necessary to achieve the library's goals and that enhance the library's ability to compete
Create a set of job "specifications"	Determine which abilities, competencies, and skills are necessary to produce outstanding performance in any particular job function (e.g., flexibility, openness to change, the ability and desire to learn and change)
Find the person who best "fits" the job	Determine which combination of resources—internal or external—provides the best strategic approach to your staffing needs, rather than specific people
Look mainly for technical competence (e.g., an MLS, five years' experience)	Find people who are more than simply "technically" qualified and can carry forward your library's mission and values; look at what they've done in those five years and whether it meets the experience, not the years, you need
Base the hiring decision primarily on the selection interview	View the selection interview as only one of a series of tools designed to make the best choice in hiring

TASK 2: DESCRIBE THE JOB

Task 1: Assess Required Staff Resources
Task 2: Describe the Job
    Step 2.1: Plan the project
    Step 2.2: Job analysis
    Step 2.3: Write job descriptions
    Step 2.4: Obtain approval and communicate
Task 3: Identify the Right Person for the Right Job
Task 4: Develop and Implement a Performance Management System
Task 5: Develop and Implement a Retention Plan

In this task, you'll learn how to focus on a library classification and describe it in detail. Depending on the number of employees your library has or needs, a job may have a single incumbent in its classification or many. Understanding what you want a person or persons to accomplish in a job is crucial to making effective hiring or appointment decisions (see chapter 4 for the details and processes of hiring or selecting a person to fill a vacant position), managing performance (see chapter 5), and retaining a loyal, productive workforce (see chapter 6). Understanding a job requires analyzing the job and then creating a job description.

Step 2.1
Plan the Project

If you are going to complete this task, refer back to the "Planning to Plan" section of chapter 1. This information will help you plan the project, determine whether you need a committee and, if so, select committee members, create a charge, and formulate a communications plan.

Step 2.2
Job Analysis

In the last chapter, you learned how to take a close look at what resources and skill sets are needed to implement your strategic plan or to develop organizational competencies. You learned how to conduct a gap analysis to determine what knowledge, skills, and abilities you need and the number of employees necessary to carry out the identified activities.

If you are developing job descriptions for current, vacant, or new positions and did not complete the gap analysis in chapter 2, start by considering what needs to be accomplished by the person or people in the job. Think about the results the person or people in the job will be expected to produce. Be sure that the job descriptions you write reflect the activities employees are currently carrying out, as well as any new activities they will be undertaking as part of implementing your strategic plan or developing organizational competencies.

Job analysis is typically conducted as a means of gathering information about jobs so that accurate job descriptions can be written. Job analysis involves carefully and systematically acquiring information about the work that is done, the level of complexity of the duties performed, the amount and kind of supervision exercised or received, the responsibilities of the job, the education, training, skills, and experience needed, and the physical and mental requirements of the work.

It's important to prepare library staff for the job analysis process. Both the jobs being studied and the managers of these jobs need to understand what the job analysis process is—and what it isn't. Staff are often concerned that a job analysis project means that jobs will be eliminated and that they will lose their jobs. This is usually not the case. It's important to reassure them that this is a process designed to identify the work being performed so that it can be described accurately in a job description. It's also important to inform staff that job analysis is not about how much work an individual is doing or how well they are doing it. If those issues exist, they should be dealt with through workload studies and the performance management process (see chapter 5). One final message to convey to staff is that a job analysis does not mean that employees will get a raise. Compensation studies address pay and benefits issues and may result in pay increases for some or many staff, depending on the findings of the study and the library's resources.

The job analysis process generally includes the following stages:

1. Employees fill out position description questionnaires (PDQs—defined below), noting the major job tasks performed and the percentage of time spent on each one.
2. PDQs are reviewed by the immediate supervisor for accuracy and completeness; areas of discrepancy or where additional information is needed are noted.

3. Employees or employee groups may be interviewed to be sure job duties and responsibilities are clearly understood.
4. Employee work locations may be visited and employees may be asked to demonstrate their job duties.

Figure 14 provides dos and don'ts for job analysis, reiterating some of the points made above. A more detailed discussion of job analysis and job descriptions is found in *Designing a Compensation Plan for Your Library*.[1]

FIGURE 14

Dos and Don'ts of Job Analysis

Do	Don't
• List the types of duties/tasks performed • Describe the level of difficulty/complexity • Identify the skills and competencies required to do the job (interpersonal communication, problem solving, persuasive skills) • Describe the kinds and quantity of contacts (personal, organizational) required by the job • Explain the level of discretion vs. following established procedures, policies, or guidelines • Describe the supervision received and exercised • Define the scope of the work to be performed • Describe the consequences of error, if any • Provide details about the amount of training and education required for the job • Describe the physical effort required, if any	• Include exhaustive listings of job duties • Provide details about the amount of work a person does. Workload is an issue to be addressed elsewhere. • Describe how well an employee is doing the work. Job performance is an issue to be addressed through the performance management process. • Discuss the perceived "importance" of the work • Include justifications for receiving a pay increase

---

Position Description Questionnaires

Position description questionnaires are typically the starting point in job analysis. If your library is part of a larger jurisdiction, such as a city or county, you may very likely have a form that you will be expected to use. If not, you can find various examples in books on the topic or on HR websites. You may also use Workform 3, Position Description Questionnaire, as the framework for your analysis. In any case, you need to make sure that the PDQ used adequately addresses the job components important to your library. If customer service is a key focus, for example, make sure employees have an opportunity to describe the customer service-related duties necessary in their jobs.

As you can see, the workform asks employees to describe the work they do in terms of the overall purpose of their job, the major activities they perform, and the percentage of time spent on each activity. Employees are also asked to identify the level of supervision they receive or exercise, the equipment and computer software they use, the education and experience they think is required to perform the job in a satisfactory manner, and the physical and environmental conditions under which they work. Some staff will find this process easier than others. Staff with jobs that have cyclical responsibilities, such as children's librarians who manage the summer reading program, or fiscal staff who manage budget preparation, may find this process particularly difficult. There is more information on estimating the amount of time required to accomplish activities in *Staffing for Results: A Guide to Working Smarter.*[2]

The challenge is to have a form that asks enough questions and provides sufficient guidance to the employee filling it out to ensure an accurate picture of the work required in the job, but not having a form so long that the employee is discouraged from taking the time to fill it out completely and thoughtfully. It may take up to an hour for an employee to fill out the PDQ, depending on the complexity of the job. Be sure to clarify that work time can be used to fill out the form.

Supervisor Reviews

After employees have filled out the forms, their immediate supervisors review the forms and note any areas of incompleteness, inaccuracy, or differences of opinion about emphasis. This review (which is supplied in a separate area on the form) provides an additional view of the work and may identify areas where the supervisor and employee do not agree on the expectations of the job. If work is changing or the library's priorities have changed, the supervisor and the employee may have different views. It's important that the supervisors and managers who review the forms take the time to carefully document any errors, omissions, or differences they perceive.

Employee Interviews

Another step in job analysis is to interview employees or groups of employees performing the same job in order to ask additional questions, clarify any differences between PDQs filled out by employees in the same job classification, or further investigate differences between what the employee and supervisor report as the employee's job duties.

Interviewing might be conducted by an HR analyst working for the city or county, by an HR analyst who works for the library itself, by a manager working for the library, or by an outside consultant hired to conduct the job analysis and write new job descriptions. Regardless of who does the interviewing and writing, the person must be someone that both library management and library employees view as knowledgeable and impartial. Since the purpose of job analysis is to gain as thorough and accurate a view of the job duties as possible, it will save time if the person doing this is conversant with library terminology and understands typical library work processes, though this is not absolutely essential. Well-trained HR professionals are skilled at analyzing work processes and asking questions that result in an accurate picture of the work being done by library employees at all levels.

For newly created positions, there may be no current incumbent and therefore no one to complete a PDQ or interview. In these cases, have the supervisor or department manager of the new position develop a PDQ for that position so that analysis may be completed and a new position description written.

Step 2.3
Write Job Descriptions

Once the PDQs are reviewed and any necessary interviews have been conducted, the work of writing job descriptions begins. The trend is toward writing broader rather than narrower, more specific job descriptions. These broader, more generic descriptions provide greater flexibility to both the employee and library. Take a look at the current ratio of job descriptions to employees in your library. Some libraries with narrowly written job descriptions find themselves with almost as many job descriptions as employees. If you have narrowly defined job classifications and job descriptions, ask yourself, "Do I really need to differentiate between Branch Clerk II, Circulation Clerk II, and Technical Services Clerk II?" You and your employees will have more flexibility in terms of job assignments, cross-training, and addressing workload issues if you create broader job titles and descriptions. In addition, this broader look at job descriptions will reduce the tendency of employees to request a reclassification or to balk at doing certain tasks because they are "not in my job description." Broadly written job descriptions will also enable you to undertake new activities as priorities change without having to rewrite job descriptions, which can be a long, drawn-out process, particularly if your library is part of a larger jurisdiction or is unionized.

Use the gap analysis you've conducted or the thinking you've done to describe the knowledge, skills, abilities, and competencies you will require for the jobs you're describing. You may find that some will be required for many or even all jobs ("Ability to establish and maintain effective working relationships with other staff and work as a team" is an example), while others will be more job-specific ("Ability to safely operate relevant cleaning equipment and safely use chemical cleaning products," for example). This is your opportunity to delineate requirements that support your library's values ("Ability to learn and practice the principles of intellectual freedom" for staff in support positions, and "Thorough knowledge of principles and practices of intellectual freedom and the Library Bill of Rights" for librarians) or the new activities you've selected ("Ability to create and present training on the use of library computers and databases for audiences with a variety of levels of technical background and skill").

Figure 15 includes a list of sample job titles for a smaller library operating from a single building, as well as for a medium-sized library with one or more branches. As you review the job titles in figure 15 and in your own library, be aware that titles can carry emotional, professional, and organizational impact. Titles like *manager, supervisor, administrator,* or *coordinator* should be used consistently and have a meaning that is understood consistently. If your library uses titles like Branch Head or Branch Operations Supervisor, will employees and the public understand what these titles mean? Will they know who is in charge? Be sure you have created internal and external (to other county or city jobs, for example) alignment in order to avoid confusion and to provide clear career paths for your employees. In addition, don't change titles lightly. Employees become attached to and identify personally with titles. While a Circulation Supervisor and a Circulation Specialist II may perform the exact same duties, the change in title can feel very much like a demotion or even an insult to employees who hold the title.

If your library is part of a city or county, you may need to use terms like *department, division,* and *unit* in a very specific way, as well as understand the nuanced differences among terms like *specialist, coordinator,* and *manager.* In the IT arena in particular, library

FIGURE 15
Sample Job Titles

Small or Medium Library	Large Library
Page	Page
Circulation Clerk	Circulation Clerk I (entry-level)
Circulation Supervisor	Circulation Clerk II (three years' experience)
Library Assistant	Circulation Supervisor
Librarian	Library Assistant I (entry-level with AA degree)
Manager (adult services, technical services)	Library Assistant II (three years' experience)
Branch Manager (large branch) or Department Head	Librarian I (entry-level, MLS)
Assistant Director	Librarian II (MLS, two years' experience)
Library Director	Manager I (small branch or central library department)
	Manager II (larger branch or central library department)
	Division Head (technical services, head of branches)
	Assistant Director
	Library Director

employees are often dismissed as less technically competent because of outdated job titles and job descriptions. Many libraries still refer to their employees as "computer op-erators" while others in their jurisdictions doing similar work have become "network analysts"—who are often paid quite a bit more.

You may have a job description format that you must follow, or you may be in the position of developing your own. If you wish, use Workform 4, Job Description Template, to develop your job descriptions. Whatever format is used, it should contain these elements:

Job title

Exemption status—exempt or nonexempt (pertains to Fair Labor Standards Act)

Reporting relationships (optional; some job descriptions include this, but others don't because the library doesn't want to be locked into a fixed organizational structure or be forced to update job descriptions each time a change is made in the organizational structure)

Job summary (one or two sentences that explain the purpose of the job)

Essential duties and responsibilities (essential functions, per the Americans with Disabilities Act; see the explanation of this in the text below)

Education/experience/certification requirements

Skills, abilities, and competencies required

Supervisory responsibility

Disclaimer statement ("Other duties as assigned" and the fact that the job description is not intended to be inclusive of all possible duties. A statement such as the following could be included: "Functions listed are intended only as illustrations of the various types of work performed. The omission of specific duties does not exclude them from the position if the work is similar, related, or a logical assignment to the position.")

Dates and approvals (by supervisor and HR)

Working conditions and physical factors (per the Americans with Disabilities Act)

The information you've gathered from the job analysis should provide all you need to fill in the required elements of the job description.

Figure 16 is a job description for a Library Clerk at the Tree County Library. Note the "disclaimer" at the end of this job description. Wording like this should be included to remind supervisors and employees that jobs change and situations change. All duties performed by an employee cannot and should not be captured in the job description.

Two of the elements included in the list above require special attention. Fair Labor Standards Act (FLSA) exemption designations are important because a position that is "exempt" is not subject to the FLSA overtime or compensatory time requirements, which state that a person working over forty hours a week must be paid time and a half or given compensatory time off for the time over forty hours worked. A position that is "nonexempt" is covered by the FLSA requirements. Executive, professional, administrative, and other highly paid workers are exempt, but the requirements are complex and designations should be made carefully. In some libraries, librarians are designated as "exempt" but in others they are not and do receive overtime or compensatory time pay. Consult with an expert in FLSA requirements to be sure that you are complying with the requirements of the FLSA law.

The second element that requires special attention is the one that refers to "essential duties and responsibilities." Care must be taken to think through what duties and responsibilities are essential because the Americans with Disabilities Act says a qualified individual is one "who, with or without reasonable accommodation, can perform the essential functions of the employment position that such individual holds or desires." The "essential functions" are those basic duties that are central to a job and cannot normally be transferred to another position or person without disruption in the flow or process of work. For example, if your stacks are in a basement without an elevator, climbing steps is an essential function for a page. However, climbing steps might not be an essential function for a reference librarian.

When writing the "essential duties and responsibilities" component of the job description, remember:

Focus on primary, required, current, normal duties and responsibilities of a classification. The list should be descriptive and representative, not exhaustive.

The statements should be discrete, identifiable aspects of the work assignment, described in one to three sentences, and should specify the expected results, allowing for alternate means of performing the duty, changes in technology, preferences of employees and supervisors, and accommodations for workers with disabilities, without altering the nature of the duty itself.

FIGURE 16
Sample Job Description

Tree County Library
JOB DESCRIPTION

Library Clerk

Grade: 2

FLSA: Non-Exempt

Date: 05/05

Job Summary: Performs a variety of routine clerical tasks to support library operations; performs other duties as assigned.

Essential Functions

1. Answers phones, greets and directs customers to appropriate areas
2. May
   - perform circulation duties such as checking materials in and out, registering customers for library cards and providing orientation to library use, calculating and collecting fines and fees
   - assist customers by locating and retrieving materials and demonstrating and providing instruction in the use of library equipment, including computers
   - reshelve materials and revise shelves as needed
   - process ILL requests, holds for customers, and orders for materials
   - perform clerical duties such as typing, filing, copying, or sorting and distributing mail
   - calculate and maintain daily, monthly, and yearly statistics
   - maintain, order, and receive supplies from vendors and distribute to branches and departments
   - strip, clean, and process a/v materials and containers for reuse
   - send old magazines to be bound for library's collection
3. Performs other duties as assigned

Required Knowledge, Skills, and Abilities

Ability to
   - gain working knowledge of TCL's policies and procedures
   - act as a representative of TCL to the public
   - learn the current shelving system
   - learn to operate relevant computer systems, including hardware and software, and simple office machines
   - perform basic math functions

Education and Experience

1. High School diploma or GED
2. Six months to one year of related experience
3. Or equivalent technical training, education, and/or experience

Physical and Environmental Conditions:

Work requires no unusual demand for physical effort.

Work environment involves everyday risks or discomforts which require normal safety precautions typical of such places as libraries, offices, or meeting and training rooms, e.g., use of safe workplace practices with office equipment, avoidance of trips and falls, and observance of fire and building safety regulations.

The above job description is not intended as, nor should it be construed as, exhaustive of all responsibilities, skills, efforts, or working conditions associated with this job.

Reasonable accommodations may be made to enable qualified individuals with disabilities to perform the essential functions of this job.

This and all library positions are eligible for systemwide transfer.

The "essential duties and responsibilities" statement typically contains three parts:

1. *Verb.* Should be action-oriented, not profession-specific.
2. *Object.* What the verb is performing action on.
3. *Purpose.* What result is achieved?

Example: Library Clerk II: Assist customers by locating and retrieving materials, and demonstrating and providing instruction in the use of library equipment, including computers.

Job descriptions also indicate the knowledge, skills, abilities, education, and experience required to do the job. This is an area where inadvertent discrimination can occur. The educational requirement must be a real necessity for the job. If the work could be accomplished by someone with equivalent job experience but who lacks a specific credential or degree, the job description should contain an "equivalency statement." For example, the job description for a technical services paraprofessional might list qualifications in this manner:

1. Associate of Arts degree from an accredited college. AA in Library Technology preferred.
2. Two years of library experience, including experience in a technical services environment utilizing specialized cataloging and acquisitions software.
3. Or equivalent technical training, education, and/or experience.

Your library or local jurisdiction probably requires job descriptions. They are traditionally part of good HR management practice, since they spell out the job duties, reporting relationships, skills, experience, and educational requirements of a job. To ensure that job descriptions are strategic tools which assist rather than hinder you in accomplishing your objectives, you want to be sure that they adequately reflect the activities you want carried out by your library's employees.

Step 2.4
Obtain Approval and Communicate

Once the job descriptions have been created, the final step is to obtain the required sign-offs and approvals. Again, what needs to be done will vary by jurisdiction. The important thing to remember is that it must be done. The finalized job descriptions may have to be approved or become official parts of a personnel system. Often this approval or acceptance date is printed on the job description itself so everyone knows that the version before them is official. A dated copy also serves as a way to keep track of how old the job description is.

Refer back to the communications plan you developed as part of the "planning to plan" process outlined in chapter 1. Everyone involved in the job description development process needs to receive notification that the process has been completed. Employees who have filled out PDQs, been interviewed, participated in discussions of draft job descriptions, or have otherwise been involved in the process will want to know that it has, at last, been completed. If the process took place as part of a negotiated agreement, union officials will also want to know that the agreed-upon activities have been concluded. Remember that anything that impacts an employee's work life is potentially sensitive. Take the time to explain what has happened and why at the end of the process, just as you did at the beginning and during the process. Time spent on this now will mean not having to spend even more time later correcting misunderstandings or partial understandings of the process and its outcome.

Notes

1. Paula Singer, *Designing a Compensation Plan for Your Library* (Chicago: American Library Association, 2002).
2. Diane Mayo and Jeanne Goodrich, *Staffing for Results: A Guide to Working Smarter* (Chicago: American Library Association, 2002), 52–53.

Chapter 4

The Right Person for the Right Job

MILESTONES

By the time you finish this chapter you will be able to

- determine whether you should recruit for a position internally, externally, or both
- enumerate and evaluate recruitment techniques and strategies
- screen and test candidates
- identify the best interview technique to use for a position
- interview top candidates
- select the right person for the job

The job market today is more competitive than it's ever been. Many workers in the public library workforce are nearing retirement age. The pool of younger workers is smaller than that of the Baby Boomer generation, so employers will be faced with the dual situation of an unprecedented number of openings and a smaller pool of potential candidates. This situation is shared by all government, business, corporate, nonprofit, and not-for-profit employers. It is magnified for libraries and others in the government and not-for-profit sectors, however, since Generation Xers appear to have been less inclined to major in subjects relevant to those sectors and less inclined to seek work in those sectors (see chapter 6 for an explanation of generational differences). Consequently, libraries are finding that they must compete aggressively to find and hire qualified candidates for their positions.

In this chapter you'll learn how to find the person you need. The "finding" may involve an internal search for the person with the right knowledge, skills, abilities, and competencies within your own library; it may involve an external search outside your library organization; or it may involve both.

TASK 3: IDENTIFY THE RIGHT PERSON FOR THE RIGHT JOB

Once you've described what you want from a position and the person in it, you will start the process of finding qualified candidates for the position. Recruitment specialists call this process "sourcing." It's an active process involving directors, managers, and other staff members. Your past experience with this step may have been placing advertisements in print or online locations (if recruiting externally) or on bulletin boards (if recruiting within the library) and waiting to see what responses came in. Much more (and a much different) effort is needed now because the hiring environment (both within the library world and the larger world of work) is so competitive and because you need to be more involved in hiring decisions that help move your library in the direction it needs to go.

Step 3.1
Plan the Project

If you are going to complete this task, refer back to the "Planning to Plan" section of chapter 1. This information will help you plan the project, determine whether you need a committee and, if so, select committee members, create a charge, and formulate a communications plan.

Step 3.2
Recruit Candidates

Effective sourcing entails developing a recruitment strategy. This strategy should be a plan for when and where to look for qualified applicants, as well as actions that can be taken to develop applicants (such as internships or on-the-job training opportunities) or relationships with people who could become applicants. It's an ongoing process, not just something that happens when there is a job opening. Library managers should always be thinking about where they could find applicants and use every opportunity to showcase the library and the community as an attractive, desirable place to work.

Internal and External Recruiting

One of the first decisions that will need to be made is whether a particular recruitment will be internal (recruiting from within the existing library workforce) or external (recruiting from outside the library). You may decide to do both. Whatever you do will be shaped by your existing procedures, policies, city or county policies if your library is part of a larger jurisdiction, and labor contracts, if applicable, all of which could influence the choices you have. Your recruitment choices will also be influenced by the position you are filling. The local labor market will probably be able to produce a number of qualified applicants for a driver or clerical position. If you are looking for someone who can catalog in a non-Romance language, however, you will probably have to look beyond the local market and recruit regionally or even nationally to find the combination of skills and experience you require. The size of the region may also vary: it could be several cities, a county or several counties, or even several states, such as the Pacific Northwest or New England.

It makes sense to recruit from the existing workforce if existing employees are known to have the skills, abilities, expertise, and competencies being sought. Job announcements can be posted on bulletin boards, in newsletters and on employee intranet sites, sent via e-mail, and in other ways that the library typically uses to disseminate information internally. Of course, all existing civil service procedures, collective bargaining agreements, and personnel policies will have to be followed in all internal recruitments.

Internal recruitment is typically less expensive and is faster than external recruitment. The candidates are known to the library, and the library and the positions being recruited for are probably known and understood by the candidates. Another real advantage is that internal recruitment is popular with employees because it provides them with opportunities for advancement. To maintain these advantages, the library employer must ensure that fair and open selection procedures are followed. If there is any sense of favoritism or other inappropriate actions, the process can result in resentment and dissent among other employees.

It is often a good idea to recruit both internally and externally. This allows internal candidates an opportunity to move up within the organization, while also giving the library the opportunity to cast its nets more widely to find a group of candidates with the best possible skills and experience to meet the library's needs. If internal candidates are selected, they have the satisfaction of knowing that they were compared with a variety of people with similar skills. If external candidates are selected, the internal candidates can usually recognize that the external candidates brought unique or enhanced skills to the positions being filled.

An external search will be necessary if it is determined that the qualifications needed for the position are not found within the library's current workforce. The extent of the search will depend upon the skills and qualifications required and the library's assessment of where those might be found. For top managerial and specialized professional and technical positions, the search might be national.

Sourcing Techniques and Strategies

Your goal should be to hire the best people for the openings your library has. To do this, you need to attract the attention of the best, so that you get a chance to tell them about the job and your library. Hiring specialist Lou Adler makes an insightful distinction when he points out that there is a fundamental difference between the best candidates and ordinary candidates. He provides several rules to follow:[1]

> To find the best people, you have to use different techniques than you would use to find ordinary people.
>
> Candidates will only explore career opportunities that meet their personal needs.
>
> The best people want careers, not jobs.

The best candidates for your jobs are not just looking for any job; in fact, they might not be actively seeking a new job at all. They will only be enticed if they see that your job provides something extra: a new challenge or opportunity for professional growth, or a step in their career that they see as significant to them. All of your interactions, from the job advertisement to the application and selection process, must be designed to interact with the candidate and provide information that he or she will need to make a decision about whether or not to work for your library.

There are three broad categories of job candidates:

Active candidates. These candidates are actively looking for another job. They need one because they don't have one or because they want to leave the one they have. This is an easy group to attract, but experienced recruiters don't view this group as a pool of top candidates. There may be some great people in the pool, but there will also be many average or even unqualified candidates. Lou Adler estimates that this group represents 10–15 percent of the total labor pool.[2]

Semi-active candidates. These are candidates who are currently employed. They may be looking for a new job periodically, especially if they've had a series of bad days and want a different environment or challenge. They may feel frustrated by their supervisor, peers, or work environment, or they may feel underappreciated, overworked, or underpaid. They don't have much time to look for another job and need to be enticed by the potential of finding another job that is significantly better than the one they currently have. Adler estimates that this group is much larger, 30–40 percent of the labor pool. This is the sourcing "sweet spot," the spot you should aim for with your ads, contacts, and recruitment and selection processes.

Passive candidates. These are people who are currently employed and don't know they want another job. They like their jobs enough that they aren't looking. However, recruiters know that up to 80 percent of these people would be open to exploring a new opportunity if someone (a recruiter or hiring manager) called them directly and talked to them about an open position. These are often very high-quality candidates, but they are expensive to woo. Because they aren't looking for a new position, considerable effort must be exerted to interest them in the job. Paid, professional recruiters are often used to find these candidates and interest them in the job. If offered the job, passive candidates will often seek a compensation package that is higher than that sought by semi-active candidates. However, for top managerial positions and library director positions at large libraries, recruiting the passive candidate is often the route that is taken to ensure that there is a pool of top-quality candidates.

Recruitment Techniques and Strategies

Bearing in mind the different kinds of candidates, what recruiting techniques are available to you? There are a variety of options including job advertisements or announcements, conferences or job fairs, employee referrals, networking, and direct contact.

JOB ADVERTISEMENTS OR ANNOUNCEMENTS

The job advertisement should be based on a current job description (for more information on creating these documents, see chapter 3). You may be constrained by library requirements or those of your parent jurisdiction (city, county, etc.), but try to make the advertisement as enticing as possible. Reciting the dry language of the job description will attract only the active candidate. To attract the semi-active job seeker, you need to write an ad with a catchy title or lead line: "Are you ready to lead a highly respected library into an era of new excellence?"

You want to include verbiage that will key in to the motivations of the semi-active job seeker. Describe the challenges and growth opportunities of the job, provide details about what the person obtaining the job will be able to do, learn, or become, and include the attractions of the location of the job and community that may appeal to personal interests: "Can you enjoy living with sunshine and the natural beauty of the nearby Rocky Mountains?" You may also want to comment on the reputation of the library or parent jurisdiction: "Are you able to guide a historically successful library in responding to the service needs of an increasingly multilingual and multicultural city?" (The quotations cited are from an e-mail sent out to attract interest and referrals for the city librarian position in Denver, Colorado.)[3]

The job advertisement should also describe critical skills required for the position and how they would be used. For example, a recruitment brochure for the library director position in Arlington, Virginia, indicated that the new director would be leading countywide initiatives on the cable channel and website as examples of why the ideal candidate must have had success working with other departments of local government in planning and managing integrated services.

Your job announcement should include the following: why the position is attractive enough for someone to leave their current one; something enticing about the library's location (such as natural beauty, sports, recreational, or cultural opportunities); a compelling description of the challenges facing the person who will fill the position; a description of the major responsibilities; reporting relationships (both who the incumbent will report to and the departments or number of staff she will manage); budget responsibility; partnerships; salary range and potential opportunities; and other perquisites or benefits such as a team-based work environment, flexible hours, free parking, great health benefits, and so on.

The job ad may be posted on the library's intranet or on job boards; sent to other libraries, e-mail lists, organizations, or library schools; or used as the basis of an individual pitch, in person or by phone or e-mail. A brochure or even a CD may be developed, providing a creative opportunity to describe the job, the library, and the service community. Some libraries have even created non-job-specific brochures to distribute at conferences or job fairs as a way to present themselves and seek candidates for future openings. To reach minority candidates, consider how people live and participate in your community. You might need to notify minority churches and colleges or specific business associations about job openings.

You might also want to think about your library's web presence. Does it only provide information about current openings? Would it be worthwhile to create information telling prospective employees what kinds of jobs the library has, how exciting and fulfilling it is to work there, how to find out when there are openings, and what the application and screening process is? Studies have shown that younger adults and minorities make heavy use of online information about jobs. If you want to attract them to the library, you need to find ways to reach them using the tools that they naturally use. Figure 17 provides an illustration of how one company used web recruitment effectively.

FIGURE 17
Web Recruitment

PriceWaterhouseCooper, a top accounting firm, has developed an exceptionally creative website (www.pwcglobal.com/lookhere/) designed to recruit young college graduates to their company. The site makes accounting sound positively exhilarating by combining images, words, and even music to appeal to the next generation of CPAs and auditors. The navigation bar on the side of their page uses phrases like:

- What did others bring?
- Propel your career
- Meet great people
- Get cool assignments
- Learn every day
- Find WorkLife

The website also shows that the firm has been named a Fortune 100 Best Company to Work For, has been voted a #1 Ideal Employer, and has been named by *Working Mother* to its Top 100 list for ten straight years in a row.

The company's commitment to work/life balance is summed up by this entry on its recruiting page: "Life is friends, memories, new experiences and lots of stuff. That stuff defines who you are and how you are unique. You should be able to bring all that with you when you start your career."

CONFERENCES AND JOB FAIRS

Large libraries often send staff members to recruit at state, regional, and national conferences. They staff a table, provide materials about their library, and discuss current or potential openings with prospective candidates. If the conference hosts an employment area or placement center, library staff will also be able to review the resumes of applicants and schedule interviews with candidates. Even if your library doesn't recruit formally at a conference, you should take advantage of being with so many colleagues to distribute information about your library and any openings you have and to meet with active and semi-active candidates. You should always be actively assessing the people you meet. Are you impressed with a fellow committee member or someone you've seen present at the conference? Try to meet them and exchange contact information. You might also want to talk to them about their career interests and let them know about current and future opportunities at your library.

Be as proactive as possible. Perform screening interviews on the spot (even if you aren't formally recruiting or using the job center) and follow up with a telephone interview if a candidate seems promising, or invite a prospect to visit the library to learn more about it and any positions that are available.

Remember, too, that a conference is a great place to showcase your library. If your library is seen as a leader and as progressive, innovative, and creative because of its visibility through conference presentations and articles in professional journals, strong candidates will want to be affiliated with you. Libraries with strong national reputations typically report that they have dozens, if not hundreds, of applications for their openings. People who are tops want to be with the best.

Job fairs may or may not be cost-effective, depending on the positions you have available. Local job fairs, especially those sponsored by organizations that are interested in equal opportunity, may be a good place to find candidates from groups that are underrepresented on your library staff. Just being at the job fair says that your library is interested in having a staff that is representative of the community as a whole. People may never have thought of applying to the library if they haven't seen others like themselves working there. It's obviously a great opportunity to inform candidates of the types of jobs available, job requirements, and the selection process. Job or career fairs and conferences are also designed for certain professions or fields (such as high tech), so become aware of these opportunities to find candidates in such specialty areas as information technology, public relations, marketing, finance, and human resources management.

Whichever type of job fair you attend, be sure to use the time there wisely. Staff your table, but also be sure to mingle with attendees. Have hiring managers available so that people can discuss real jobs with them and so that they can engage the top candidates. Think of a gimmick or giveaway (a CD about your library, or a free book with a library bookplate or travel coffee mug) that will attract people to your booth and serve as a reminder of how to contact you later. You might also consider holding a drawing to give away an item of greater value so that you can get cards from potential applicants. Then you can follow up with those applicants after the job fair.

EMPLOYEE REFERRALS

One of the best sources for candidates for your open positions or future open positions is the people who already work for your library. Ask staff to talk up the library with family, friends, neighbors, and those in their religious, civic, youth, sports, or service organizations. Train staff members to talk about the library in a clear, crisp, and compelling way. While your library's nepotism policy would probably forbid employees working directly for family members, employees are a wonderful source of potential candidates.

Why are staff so important? They know the culture, the work, and the institution best and can serve as reliable screeners. This can be a particularly effective way to boost your diversity hiring, since the staff you have will know others in the ethnic, racial, linguistic, and other groups you'd like to see work for you. One large urban library is a model in this regard. That library's minority professional staff has consistently remained at 20 percent due to thoughtful, proactive recruitment efforts.

Make the process of employee referrals a formal activity, heavily promoted throughout the library. Let your employees know that you value their suggestions and will follow up quickly to make contact with people they recommend to you. Ask staff to give you names and contact information. Your HR department or hiring managers can then follow up by providing potential applicants with the details of the job and the testing or selection process that will be followed to fill the job.

NETWORKING

Take every opportunity to find and cultivate potential candidates. Besides being visible at conferences through presentations, meet and talk with colleagues at programs, receptions, and through your involvement on committees and organizational boards. If your community is large enough to have a local library association, get involved and get to know your colleagues. A top candidate may be working at a local academic, school, or special library. Don't let the experience they have at another type of library be a barrier to considering what skills they could bring to your library. Review the job descriptions you've prepared so that you know what knowledge, skills, abilities, and past accomplishments you are looking for.

Use the top candidates you find to suggest other top candidates. Top performers recognize other top performers. They may have worked with them, been on an association committee with them, or admired their work from afar. As you talk with people and describe the challenges and opportunities for growth and development in your library, ask them for the names of others that they feel are exceptional performers in their area of expertise or specialization. For example, the best source for information about qualified technical services managers would be others who are specialists in that area. Don't ask if the people they refer are looking for a job; just ask for additional names that could be used as resources for you. Ask what they admire about the people they suggest, and ask about their qualifications. That can serve as an initial screening before you decide whether or not it will be cost-effective for you to follow up. If you do follow up, you'll already have some good information as a basis for an exploratory conversation with the next person, ending again by asking for additional names.

Figure 18 provides some interesting techniques that other professions have employed to recruit successfully for new employees.

FIGURE 18
What Can We Learn from Other Professions?

Libraries aren't the only institutions facing recruitment challenges. As Baby Boomers retire, all facets of the public sector as well as private employers will be facing a huge drain of employees. Every sector will be competing for new employees. Here are a few ideas a library could consider:

The FBI, after years of failing to attract minority candidates (the FBI is 83% white and 83% male), decided to ask the peers of targeted recruits (i.e., minority college students) to assist them.

Students at Morgan State University in Baltimore (a historically black college) used the $2,500 granted to them to come up with a recruitment campaign using the theme "The FBI: Keeping It Fresh, Bold and Innovative" and campaign ads that featured students on campus. They also hosted "FBI fun nights" where real agents and their families met with college students in a relaxed setting.

Clark Atlantic, another historically black college, held a mixer at a soul food eatery. Students at both schools learned about the array of specialties in the bureau. These campaigns resulted in 330 new bureau applications from minorities for an array of jobs, ranging from investigator to financial analyst.

The Oregon Center for Nursing, after projecting that one in five nursing positions in Oregon would be unfilled by 2010, developed a campaign to attract more men to the field (only 11% of Oregon nurses are male; nationally the figure is even lower at 5%).

Defying the stereotype of a white woman in a white cap, the OCN came up with a testosterone-drenched campaign: "Are you man enough . . . to be a nurse?" The accompanying ads and posters feature nine macho men, including a Harley rider, a black belt, a combat medic, a snowboarder, and a rugby player.

Other states have replicated the campaign. The OCN and other groups feature pictures of men and of men and women of color performing a variety of interesting duties on their websites, along with inspiring quotations about the value and gratification of their nursing work.

Workform 5, Recruitment Process, provides an outline for a recruitment process, including a way to track the person or group responsible for each step of the process and a way to check off each completed step. If your library or jurisdiction doesn't already have a recruitment process in place that you are required to follow, the workform provides a basic process.

Step 3.3
Screen and Test Candidates

The recruitment techniques discussed in Step 3.2 may result in many applicants. The next step in the hiring process is to screen those applicants and to arrange for testing, if that will be needed.

Screen the Applications

Applicants are typically asked to fill out an application form. They may or may not be asked to attach a resume. Care must be taken that the information requested on the application form directly relates to the job and that there are not information requests or questions that are not job-related. Inappropriate or illegal requests include those related to age, race, color, sex, religion, national origin, or physical disability, or to personal information that is not related to required employment information or potential job performance.

The information on both the application and the resume (if a resume was requested) is used to determine whether or not the candidate has met the minimum qualifications of the position during an initial screening process. This screening may or may not be a straightforward process. It's important that the person or persons doing the screening thoroughly review the job description to understand exactly what knowledge, skills, abilities, experience, and competencies will be required to perform the job effectively. Your library or jurisdiction may have specific procedures or guidelines for performing the screening, but try to be as flexible as possible. For example, people who lack the formal education listed in the job description but have indicated through their previous jobs that they can do what is required of the open job should not be screened out. You may or may not know this at the application screening process, depending on the detail of the application, the applicant's resume, and whether or not supplemental questions (discussed below) have been used.

Some libraries also include supplemental questions as part of the application process. Candidates provide written responses to the questions and submit them with their application form and resume. These questions are usually used for higher-level professional, technical (such as information technology, accounting, facilities management), and managerial positions. As with all other elements of the selection process, these questions should be job-related (the KSAs portion of the job description should be very useful in developing questions that will provide relevant job performance information) and should be evaluated in an objective, consistent manner. The answers to supplemental questions are not always used in initial screening (unless they are missing or so brief or lacking in quality that they clearly eliminate the candidate), but they may be useful in a later screening to narrow a field of candidates down to a smaller number who are then invited to interviews. If you decide to use supplementary questions, be sure that the questions are clear and pertinent to the job. If you ask a lot of supplementary questions and they are complex, some applicants may decide the job application is more trouble than it is worth.

If your library is part of a jurisdiction (such as a city or county) that manages the screening process, you must be sure that the person in the HR department assigned to screen applications has a thorough understanding of the job that is to be filled and has objective criteria based on the job description written for the job. Depending on the policies and practices of your jurisdiction, you may not have the opportunity to be as flexible in your screening as is recommended here.

Test the Candidates

Depending on the type and level of position, there may be other steps in the initial selection process. Many libraries conduct skills tests of some sort: keyboarding, demonstrations of proficiency levels using standard office word-processing and spreadsheet products, alphanumeric filing, language proficiency, and demonstrating proficiency in a key aspect of the position, such as preparing a news release or telling a story. Depending on the type of job and number of applicants, these tests may be conducted for large groups as an early screening activity, or they may be conducted later in the selection process with only those candidates who are seen as the most competitive. For example, a large library with numerous openings for page and clerical positions may conduct monthly alphanumeric filing and keyboarding skills tests. A library hiring a bilingual children's librarian might ask only the top candidates to tell a story in Spanish as part of its hiring process.

Whatever form of testing is used, it must be valid and reliable. A valid test measures factors that are job-related: alphanumeric filing for a page and clerk, keyboarding for a clerk, writing skills for an administrative assistant. To be reliable, the test must be conducted in a consistent manner. Many libraries are part of a city or county civil-service system that administers standardized tests, ranks applicants by score, and uses other means to ensure that tests are conducted in a fair, objective manner. While these approaches can add time and bureaucratic intricacies to the hiring process, they are designed to ensure that candidates are rated on merit rather than on non-job-related factors such as who they know, who they are related to, or who they support politically.

Step 3.4
Interview Candidates

Professional, technical, and managerial positions often entail an oral interview process. Depending on the library's size and structure, there may be a series of interviews held to fill a position. The first interview might be designed to rank candidates, and a subsequent interview might be the basis for the actual hiring decision. In other situations, everything might be accomplished in one interview. Sometimes a library will decide to conduct multiple interviews, perhaps because it has additional questions for the top candidates (usually this is because there are competing strengths and more information is needed) or because it wants additional people to be involved in the hiring decision. Whichever situation you find yourself in, remember to use interviewing techniques strategically, to help you find the right person for your position.

Interviewing Tips

There are some basic interviewing principles to keep in mind. You don't want to lose a strong candidate as a result of your own hiring process or by being discourteous. Remember, you are trying to attract the best and brightest, as are other library and nonlibrary organizations with which you are competing. Whereas interview advice has traditionally been directed at candidates and relates to how they should behave during an interview, the tables are turning. An equal amount of focus is now on employer behavior and processes and what the interviewer or employer can do to accommodate the candidate. Here are some tips for being proactive.

To start, always be prepared. Know the job, the reporting relationships, the performance expectations, the compensation, and the career path. From the moment the candidate walks in, establish and maintain rapport: greet her warmly and display interest throughout the interview. Remember, the interviewer is the salesperson for the job to be filled. Listen carefully to the candidate, paraphrase what she says, and summarize your understanding. Make the candidate feel heard. Provide realistic organizational and job information. Describe the library's philosophy, plans, and practices and provide a job description. If possible, also provide a tour of the library. Do not oversell the job or the library. It is what it is; however, do describe the job's challenges and growth potential. In addition, be honest about hiring salary, work environment, and culture. If the library really isn't like a "family," don't say that it is. If work hours are flexible, mention that.

At the end of the interview, summarize and preview the next steps. Tell candidates what to expect next and when you will get back to them. Always get back to the candidates when you said you would! Be nice and pleasant, even if a particular candidate isn't a good fit. The candidate may have all the qualifications and KSAs for another job that hasn't opened yet, or she may apply for a vacancy in your library five years later. Candidates will certainly talk to each other about the library and their experiences interviewing. It is always a good policy to stay on good terms and present the library's best face to candidates.

You should also be flexible. If a candidate has difficulty meeting during regular library hours, arrange for an evening or weekend interview. Non-peak-hour interviews have many advantages, including

- increased interview attendance by employed people who can't normally get away from their current job
- reduced cancellations by both candidates and managers due to last-minute work conflicts
- more time for the interview, because there's no rush to return to work
- a different approach, which makes you stand out among competitors
- making your library appear flexible to outside people (even to those who don't apply)
- increasing the number of candidates you attract, since there is more parking and less traffic after hours
- fewer interruptions by the staff of a harried manager
- increased diversity of interviewees: one parent can provide child care while the other interviews, and low-income candidates who cannot afford to miss a day of work are more likely to attend.[4]

If a candidate is from another city and your library budget doesn't support travel, consider interviewing via telephone or videoconferencing. Be sure that your paperwork for the hiring process flows easily and quickly. Don't keep a good candidate waiting for a response from you, since you don't want to lose her while you are waiting for the paper trail to catch up. Expedite your recruitment and selection processes. See how you can streamline these processes by trimming and combining several steps. *The Library's Continuous Improvement Fieldbook* offers a variety of tools for reviewing and improving work processes.[5]

Bear in mind that while you are evaluating the candidate, she is also evaluating the position and you as a potential supervisor. Do everything you can to stay on schedule. Leaving a candidate waiting for a long time is rude and discourteous. Remember that your behavior during this interview reflects directly on you and the library.

In many parts of the country and for many positions, it is a sellers' market for talent. Some Boomer and Traditionalist managers have expressed shock that GenXer and Millennial candidates even interview them. This shouldn't be a surprise, given the discussion in chapter 6 about generational differences. You need to interview and treat candidates the way they need to be interviewed and treated. So be flexible in your process, tailor it to the person being interviewed, and be cognizant of her needs and expectations regarding information, understanding of the job and the work, schedules, when she can expect a promotion, and so on.[6] Don't get angry if she asks about telecommuting, vacation days, or if her pension is portable. Answer her questions in an honest and forthright manner and you'll be assured of an employee who wants to work for your library and fits with your culture.

Interview Process

Interviewing is a selection procedure designed to predict future job performance on the basis of an applicant's responses to oral inquiries. Obviously, it's a critical part of the selection process. If the interview isn't conducted well, a person may be hired who isn't a good fit for the job. This can result in large costs (related to managing substandard performance, in addition to costs to recruit, select, and train again) if the person is terminated during the probationary period, and even larger costs if the person is kept on but is not able to perform effectively in the job. These costs relate to lost productivity and low job performance, morale problems with the person in the job and coworkers, and costs related to managing substandard performance. A poorly conducted interview might also cause a qualified candidate to decide not to take a job at the library even if the job was offered. A good interview process is a two-way street: the library is looking for the most qualified candidate for the position, and the applicants are looking for a challenging and rewarding job and work environment.

The intent of the interviewing process should be to find the candidate who is the best fit in terms of the library's organizational values, the job's objectives and specifications, the needed job skills and competencies, the library's culture, and the candidate's past performance and its relevancy to what the library needs in the current position.

Everyone involved in the interviewing process should be knowledgeable about the job's requirements. The job description is the key document to review, since it will specify the required knowledge, skills, abilities, and competencies and will provide an overview of the key responsibilities and duties of the job. Job-specific questions should be developed using the job description, and the questions should be reviewed by the hiring manager to ensure that they accurately reflect her priorities and will garner answers that indicate whether or not a candidate will be able to accomplish the activities related to the position. Be sure to focus on the entire job, not just the next big project or areas of the job that have been performed poorly in the past.

It's important that all candidates are asked the same questions during the interview process that is used to rank candidates. This ensures fairness, since all candidates will have been asked to respond to the same questions, and it also ensures that the interviewers don't jump to conclusions about candidates. Oral interviews that are conducted to rank candidates are typically the most structured, with all questions the same for each candidate, asked by the same person, within the same time frame.

Oral interviews conducted during the last stage of the hiring process (that is, designed to produce a final decision and job offer) may be less structured, using questions that are different because they are designed to follow up on information gleaned during the earlier, more structured process. For example, a library might have two final candidates for a branch manager position. As is typical, each of the candidates possesses different strengths and deficiencies. Final interview questions would be designed to probe more deeply in both areas of strength and of comparative weakness. These questions will provide the information needed to make the final decision between the two candidates.

The interview itself can include a variety of different people. It might be one-on-one between the candidate and one person representing the library. More typically, the interview will be conducted by a panel made up of the hiring manager, other interested managers, and often someone from outside the library who has expertise in an area related to the job. As noted earlier, in some cases the interview process is sequential, with the candidate being interviewed by a series of individuals or groups.

Whatever approach is used, interviewers must understand the job and what it is designed to accomplish. If the interviewers don't know the job they will substitute their own perceptions of what it is, which will lead to faulty assessments. For example, if a library is hiring a head of technical services and is looking for someone who is willing and able to streamline workflow and negotiate vendor-provided services, it's important that interviewers know this. Otherwise, they might think that the most knowledgeable cataloger among the applicants is the best candidate because that is their perception of the job, or because that's what the previous head of technical services did. However, it is quite possible that the best candidate to evaluate and streamline technical services is not someone who spends over half of her time creating detailed original records for audiovisual and foreign language materials. Clearly, the assessment of the candidate will be quite different depending on the interviewers' understanding of the job.

It's also important to consider that those who often appear to be the best candidates may not necessarily be the best person for the job. Superior job performance is the ultimate goal, not superior skills in facilely presenting oneself at the interview. A candidate may be assertive, affable, articulate, and present herself well. The interviewer must probe beyond these interview skills to find out what the candidate has actually done in her past positions and what her level of self-motivation and drive are to ascertain whether or not she will get the desired results on the job.

There are a number of approaches that can be taken to interviewing. Three approaches that would be useful to libraries are described in figure 19. You can mix and match the components, based on your needs and resources. In reality, you will probably use a combination of the interview approaches in figure 19. However, you don't want to ask too

FIGURE 19
Interviewing Approaches

	Structured	Performance-Based	Behavioral
Description	A set number of structured questions designed to elicit basic information	Questions designed to reveal actual work performance	Questions designed to describe specific situations in past jobs that demonstrate behaviors key to the open job
Questions	• Job interest • Current work status • Work experience • Educational background • Self-assessment	Describe a major project or accomplishment in depth, including • when • where • why • how • who	Tell me about a time you set a goal and were able to meet, achieve, or exceed it (link to job and behavioral competencies)
Best uses	• Interview time is limited • Position is structured • Large candidate pool	• Skilled interviewers available to tease out actual accomplishments • Library seeks talented employees rather than talented interviewees	• Library is looking for specific behaviors tied to needed knowledge, skills, and abilities (KSAs) • Time and resources are available to develop good behavioral questions based on job and organizational analysis

many questions. Your time with each applicant will be relatively limited. Focus on questions that will help you determine whether the applicants have the knowledge, skills, and abilities to do the job and to help you distinguish which of the applicants is most suited to the position you are filling.

You'll want to elicit basic information about a candidate's educational and work background, but in order to be strategic in your selection and hiring decisions, you'll want to focus on what the person has done in the past and how that can relate to what you need done at your library. Just because someone has ten years' reference or children's services experience doesn't mean she will fit into the reference or children's services environment in your library. If you're looking for someone who will be comfortable as well as creative in delivering services in a community center serving new immigrants, you need to ask questions that will elicit the information you need. Before conducting the interview, jot down a list of the attributes or abilities you will be looking for.

For example, a county library has developed a number of core and functional competencies for its library. The knowledge, skills, and abilities required to demonstrate these competencies have also been identified. The library has then created a number of interview questions that can be used as staff are hired to fill positions. In this library, a basic performance competency for all employees is the ability to provide excellent customer service. Candidates for a circulation clerk position could be asked the following questions as a way of determining their ability to provide excellent customer service:

How do you know if your customers are satisfied? Please give a specific example.

Please describe a situation when you didn't have enough time to satisfy a particular customer. How did you handle the situation?

How have you handled a dissatisfied or irate customer?

What do you think your customers would say about your work?

What should the interviewers be looking for in the answers to these questions? They would want to hear how the candidate tried to meet customers' needs, the steps she took to address their concerns, whether or not she reacted with respect, how well she appeared to listen, whether or not she allowed a customer to vent, the approach she took to identify the complaint and the steps she took to resolve the problem, as well as the follow-up she offered.

Workform 6, Developing Interview Questions, provides ideas for developing structured, performance-based, and behavioral interview questions.

Interviewing is a learned skill that improves with experience. Figure 20 provides some suggestions for effective interviewing.

Remember, too, that it is inappropriate (and illegal!) to ask questions of a personal nature. As with the application form, interview questions that cannot be asked include those about marital status, race, nationality, religious affiliation, number of children, age or date of birth or date of high school graduation, past medical problems, disabilities, number or kinds of arrests, ethnic association of surname, or veteran status. Questions must be job-related. For example, a library can state what an employee's work schedule will be and ask whether the candidate has concerns or conflicts with it. The library cannot, however, ask if the candidate has children at home or what her religion is.

In some situations, a hiring interview is held after the first qualifying interview. Whether or not this is done depends on local practice and whether or not a clear decision can be made on the basis of the first interview. If it is done, the hiring interview provides an opportunity to get to know the candidate even more and to talk about the actual job in greater depth. You will do more talking at this interview, but you will employ the same interviewing skills and follow the same dos and don'ts listed earlier. Your goal now is to zero in on determining the best talent and skill fit for your job.

There are things you must know about each candidate, and now is the time to make sure the candidate can do the entire job. Review figure 21 to make sure you have covered all your bases. For every level of job in the library, you want someone who has energy and drive and demonstrates initiative and self-motivation. Working through the checklist in figure 21 will help you determine whether or not you have found these qualities in the candidates you've interviewed. If you have, you will build an employee base that can accomplish the activities necessary for the library to achieve its goals and objectives. If too many of the needed KSAs and personal qualities are missing, you will have more personnel issues to manage and more training and development challenges to address.

FIGURE 20
Interviewing Dos and Don'ts

Dos	Don'ts
• Prepare—learn as much as you can about the job; read any materials (such as candidate applications and resumes) you're given ahead of time	• Avoid stereotyping or jumping to conclusions. Base your impressions on what you hear and what the candidate can tell you about what she has done in past positions.
• Establish rapport with the candidates—be open and friendly and help them get through their initial nervousness	• Don't make snap judgments. More hiring mistakes are made in the first thirty minutes of an interview than at any other time. Why? If our initial impression is favorable, we'll begin selling the job, magnifying the positives we hear and minimizing any negatives that come up. Conversely, if our initial impression is negative, we dismiss the candidate before we've even heard much about her accomplishments in other jobs.
• Ask the same questions of each candidate. You want to find out the same sorts of things. Using a structured set of questions and consistent types of follow-up questions will ensure that you do.	
• Listen carefully to what they have to say—ask follow-up questions but fight the urge to talk extensively yourself	
• Watch for nonverbal cues or responses that might signal evasiveness	• Be wary of the halo/horn effect. This refers to our being influenced by the last positive or negative thing we heard or, in the case of a current employee, the last job activity. All information should be taken as a whole, with no one piece carrying a disproportionate weight.
• Take notes—if there are more than a few candidates, the interviews can easily run together. You want to be sure your impressions are based on information you've gleaned on past performance, not on your superficial impressions.	
• Tell the candidates what will happen next and within what time frame. If it takes several days to conduct interviews or process results, they need to know.	• Avoid contrasting the candidate in front of you with ones you have seen previously. Take in information on each candidate and then make comparisons at the end of the interview day, after you've seen and heard them all.
• Be sure that there is follow-up. Candidates deserve the courtesy of knowing where they are in the process. If they are ranked, eliminated, or selected to move to a next step, they need to know as soon as possible.	• Avoid telegraphing answers to candidates, verbally or through your own body language. Be friendly and open but don't react to or lead the interviewee.

FIGURE 21
Things You Must Consider

☐ Level of energy, drive, initiative, self-motivation

☐ Ability to work in environment like one library will provide

☐ Motivation to do the type of work at peak levels

☐ Technical competency and ability to apply that knowledge to achieve the desired results

☐ Ability to meet all of the KSAs in the job description

☐ Ability to meet managerial, team, and organizational job responsibilities

☐ Experience and education compared to job needs

☐ Problem-solving and analytical skills using real problems as tests

☐ Accomplishments—get examples of previous projects and accomplishments

☐ Commitment and responsibility

☐ Confidence and positive attitude

By now you've described the job thoroughly and honestly, you've gone over the performance expectations, and you've heard the candidates describe their past accomplishments. You should have a good sense of their motivations and skills. You're about ready to make your selection. There is just one more process left.

Step 3.5
Check References and Make Job Offer

The long road to hiring the best person for the job is almost over, but an important, though often overlooked or minimized, step is next. You *must* contact references. Many people avoid this or think that they won't get useful information back, but it is an essential part of the hiring process. Some libraries or their parent cities or counties, afraid of lawsuits if they give unfavorable references, will only provide minimal information. On the other hand, *not* contacting references can set you up for negligent hiring claims! Hiring managers (who should be involved in this process) are often able to obtain answers to performance-based questions from references. Often the key is to label the reference as personal or confidential.

Written permission should be obtained from candidates to contact the references they have provided on their application or resume. Normally, the library will only check references for those candidates being seriously considered for the open position. It's a waste of time and energy for the library to do checking any earlier in the process, and the candidate often doesn't want his current employer to know he's job hunting until he's close to being offered a position. At that point he can inform his references, if he hasn't already done so.

Think strategically during this process. What references have been provided? Are they consistent with the job you're trying to fill? In other words, will they have knowledge of the applicant's accomplishments and the scope of his current or previous jobs? Will they be able to tell you about the job environment? References don't have to be limited to supervisors and bosses. Coworkers and even subordinates can often be excellent references because of their firsthand knowledge of the candidate's work performance and ability to interact effectively with coworkers and customers. They'll be able to describe the workload, types of customers encountered, physical challenges (such as a noisy, crowded work environment), pace of work, and quality of the library's processes and systems.

Most candidates provide as references only those who will speak highly of them personally and professionally. It is acceptable, and even advisable, to go beyond the list provided. Do call prior employers even if these are not listed by the candidate. You can Google candidates and even view their profiles on MySpace and Facebook. The library community is a small one, so contact peers, subordinates, and supervisors that you know personally or professionally for additional insight about the work and work habits of the candidate. Depending on your local situation, you may want to seek legal advice regarding contacting others not listed by the candidate as references.

Prepare for talking with references as thoroughly as you prepared for the interview with the candidate, bearing in mind that the amount of time you spend and the number of questions you ask will usually correlate to the level and complexity of the position. Ask questions of the person providing the reference to establish that person's relationship to the candidate, their title and job responsibilities. Prepare questions to ask about the candidate. There are a number of checklists available, and one is provided as Workform 7,

Reference Check Form. Customize whatever form you use to fit your own needs, and be sure to ask some questions that relate directly to the job description and KSAs you have for the position. For example, if you are hiring a circulation clerk who will be interacting with a wide variety of customers in a number of situations, you would want to ask the people providing references how they had observed the candidate handling difficult customer interactions.

A good reference interview takes time. When you call a person for a reference, start the conversation by asking if this is a good time to talk. If not, schedule an appointment with the person and call back later. As with fact-finding during the interview with the candidate, you want to get as many details and examples as you can. Don't settle for general statements ("He's terrific!"). Ask the reference to back her statements up with specifics. The reference will soon realize that you want to do more than fill in a form and will begin to open up with you. However, remember that by law, human resources departments are only required to provide confirmation that the person did indeed (or does still) work for their organization and in what position/title, unless the candidate has provided a signed release allowing additional information (such as performance) to be shared.

You need to approach reference checking with an open mind. The fact that you are checking references means that the candidates have passed an initial screening and done well in the interview process. You are already feeling positively toward the remaining candidates and you are undoubtedly contemplating the end of a long, time-consuming recruitment and selection process. You may have a candidate that you prefer, or there might be two candidates who appear to be equally qualified. You're eager to wrap things up and get the new employee in the open position. This is a potentially dangerous time for you. If you go into the reference checking with your mind made up, just looking for confirmation of the decision you've already made, you're wasting your time. Instead, you must be willing to uncover things that would cause you to change your mind or at least rethink the direction in which you're leaning. You want to continue to be objective and to remain in a fact-finding and fact-verification mode. The biggest mistake you can make is to hire someone who really isn't right for the position.

When you have finished checking references, close your files and think over your candidates. You have recruited top candidates, questioned them thoroughly, and learned how to back up your interviews with real reference checks. Now you are ready to make informed job offers with real confidence!

How you make the job offer will depend on the practices and policies of your library and its parent jurisdiction (city or county). In some cases the director or hiring manager makes the offer, while in others someone in the human resources department makes the offer. The person making the offer should be prepared to provide information about the proposed salary, benefits, and any other details such as reimbursement for moving expenses. Depending on the circumstances, there may or may not be back-and-forth negotiations around these details. The offer is usually made by phone, then followed up by a letter, which contains all the details that have been discussed verbally. If the offer is conditional based on employment eligibility being verified (for example, the candidate's right to work in the United States) or on a drug test, the candidate should be informed of these final requirements.

The candidate may want a day or two to make a final decision, which is reasonable. If all goes well and the candidate accepts your offer, the employment relationship begins, even before the new employee has begun work. The work of making sure that the employee stays with the library has started during the hiring process and will continue as the new employee is oriented to the library and her job. Chapter 6 provides information on retaining your library's best employees.

Notes

1. Lou Adler, *Hire with Your Head: Using Power Hiring to Build Great Companies,* 2nd ed. (Hoboken, NJ: John Wiley and Sons, 2002), 236.
2. Lou Adler, "The Sourcing Sweet Spot: How to Find the Best without Really Trying," The Adler Group online newsletter, May 16, 2003. http://www.adlerconcepts.com/resources/column/sourcing/the_sourcing_sweet_spot_how_to.php.
3. Recruitment for Denver city librarian conducted by Dubberly Garcia Associates, Inc., in 2006.
4. John Sullivan, "Hold Evening Interviews: Interview Candidates When They're Available," Gately Consulting, article 156, July 2001. http://ourworld.compuserve.com/homepages/GATELY/pp15js00.htm.
5. Sara Laughlin, Denise Sisco Shockley, and Ray Wilson, *The Library's Continuous Improvement Fieldbook* (Chicago: American Library Association, 2003).
6. Lynne C. Lancaster and David Stillman, *When Generations Collide* (New York: HarperCollins, 2005).

Chapter 5

Create a High-Performance Workforce

MILESTONES

By the time you finish this chapter you will be able to

- list the elements in a performance management system
- refine your current performance management system to make it more effective
- link the goals in the library's strategic plan to individual employee work plans
- write measurable employee performance activities
- provide coaching and mentoring throughout the year
- evaluate employees without committing common rating errors
- train managers and supervisors on your performance management system

If you followed the strategic planning model described in *The New Planning for Results: A Streamlined Approach,* your library went through a community-based process that ultimately developed service goals, objectives, and activities to support targeted community needs. Implementation follows the approval of the strategic plan, and the next steps would include considering the allocation of the resources necessary to execute the plan: staff, library materials, facilities, and technology.

In chapter 2 you identified the activities required to accomplish the goals of your library's strategic plan. Even if you don't have a formal strategic plan, you should have a sense of what you want to accomplish. If you've used the *Planning for Results* model, you know that your strategic plan of service is composed of goals and objectives designed to provide the services that your community needs and wants. As you contemplated what you needed to do, you probably also identified organizational competencies that needed to be developed so that you had the organizational infrastructure or institutional capacity in place to accomplish your goals. You might, for example, find that you need to completely overhaul your policies and procedures so that the activities you need to perform can be performed consistently and efficiently throughout the library. If so, a lot of information about organizing, updating, and creating policies can be found in another book in the Results series, *Creating Policies for Results: From Chaos to Clarity*.[1] All the activities related to planning and carrying out this project would be related to building organizational capacity.

The analysis of what you need, what you have, and the resulting gap or surplus hinged on identifying required knowledge, skills, and abilities. This gap analysis helped you develop a comprehensive look at your staffing needs at the work unit, department, or possibly even the entire library level. You realized that strategic staffing required looking at staffing not just as filling holes in the organization or acquiring additional staff hours to cover additional service hours or a new facility, but as a process of matching what you specifically needed to accomplish (the identified activities) with the correct number of employees possessing the correct mix of KSAs.

In chapter 3 you took the activities (the everyday work, the work required by new services or expansions of existing services, and the work required to develop organizational competence or capacity) and used them as the basis for developing or reviewing job descriptions. In chapter 4 you used your insight into what you needed, what you had, and what you wanted your employees to accomplish in their jobs to recruit and select candidates for open positions. In this chapter, you will again use the activities you've identified and the job descriptions you developed or updated to work with employees to manage their job performance.

If you used *Planning for Results* or another process for strategic planning, you will readily see the need for a performance management system. A performance management system is more than the completion of the employee's evaluation form at the end of the year; rather, it looks at performance management holistically and as part of a system that includes the following components in an ongoing process: planning, coaching, and reviewing performance, along with setting performance goals and providing feedback. A performance management system includes setting specific activities to be carried out during the performance year, day-to-day coaching and feedback among supervisors and employees, and the formal evaluation at the end of the performance year. In many ways it is the informal, ongoing process of feedback and coaching that is so important, because it helps staff keep in touch with the supervisor's and the organization's priorities and to obtain feedback about how they are performing throughout the year, rather than only at evaluation time. Using this ongoing, cyclical process of performance management allows employees to refocus their efforts as necessary or to be aware of how they may exceed the expectations set for them during the year.

An effective performance management system helps staff close the gap between what they are doing now and what they will need to do to implement the results of the strategic plan efficiently and effectively. Even if you have not engaged in strategic planning, you have goals, projects, or partnerships you want to accomplish. Following the task and steps in this chapter will help you create a performance plan to mobilize staff to accomplish what is needed, and to identify clear, relevant expectations for employees. This chapter, which builds on the activities you identified in chapters 2 and 3, will provide you with the information, models, and appraisal forms you need to implement a successful performance management system in your library.

Defining Performance Management

What is performance management? Performance management involves designing an effective process that provides coaching and feedback throughout the year, as well as assisting managers with performance appraisals and dealing with substandard job performance. Performance management includes both employee self-evaluation and supervisory evaluation. The word *system* is used to denote an ongoing process as opposed to a one-time event. The performance appraisal form, while a part of performance management and used to set performance expectations for the coming year and review the accomplishments of the current year, is but one part of a larger process, or system. The focus is on performance and results. Having an effective performance management system in place is a statement of the library's commitment to a performance-based culture, as opposed to a culture of entitlement or favoritism, where all employees get the same increase regardless of performance or where only certain employees get higher increases (based more on the supervisors' preference than on any true distinction in performance levels).

Effective performance management systems provide benefits for the library as a whole as well as for managers and employees.

> *For the library.* Performance management can help communicate your strategic goals or objectives; identify needs for training and development; build stronger working relationships; improve overall organizational productivity; provide a basis for promotions, salary increases, and other HR actions; and provide formal documentation on performance deficiencies.

> *For the manager or supervisor.* Performance management can identify high performers for advancement; identify poor performers for coaching or counseling; improve individual productivity and teamwork; identify areas for training and development; and aid in developing or improving rapport with employees.

> *For employees.* Performance management can satisfy the need to know, "How am I doing?"; allow participation in the evaluation process; encourage responsibility and accountability for performance; allow for feedback and two-way communication between employees and supervisors or managers; clarify expectations; and provide opportunities for personal and career development. Most important, the cyclical nature of the performance management system allows the employee to track her performance throughout the year with ongoing feedback from the supervisor, in order to avoid the surprise of a less-than-expected rating at the end of the performance year.

When thinking about performance management, it is essential to move away from the concept of performance management as a one-time, once-a-year event. Successful performance management is an ongoing process; ideally, some facet of performance management is occurring every day in your library. There should be no surprises at the formal review time. The strategic planning process drives the cycle and is the only component that may not occur afresh each year. The model in figure 22 illustrates the performance management cycle.

FIGURE 22
Performance Management

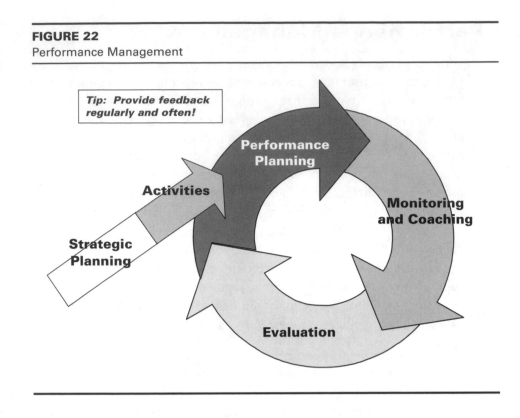

Tip: Provide feedback regularly and often!

Performance Planning

Activities

Monitoring and Coaching

Strategic Planning

Evaluation

TASK 4: DEVELOP AND IMPLEMENT A PERFORMANCE MANAGEMENT SYSTEM

Task 1: Assess Required Staff Resources
Task 2: Describe the Job
Task 3: Identify the Right Person for the Right Job
Task 4: Develop and Implement a Performance Management System
   Step 4.1: Review or develop a performance management system
   Step 4.2: Manage and monitor a performance management system
   Step 4.3: Develop individual performance plans
   Step 4.4: Monitor and coach individuals
   Step 4.5: Evaluate and rate individuals
   Step 4.6: Plan for the next cycle
Task 5: Develop and Implement a Retention Plan

Step 4.1
Review or Develop a Performance Management System

It is possible that your current performance management system does not provide all of the benefits listed in the previous section. The system you are using may not be a performance management system you designed or control, but instead the system used by the city or county in which you work. Perhaps the system you are using has been in place for years, or even decades, without review. To ensure that it is an effective system, start by reviewing the current system to see if it has the following:

An infrastructure that ensures ownership and accountability for performance at every level in the library. This includes a statement of purpose and a procedure or instructions for use as well as training and education for both employees and supervisors. It also includes the organizational understanding that the system will be used by everyone according to agreed-upon timetables. In other words, if the library believes that performance management is an essential activity, everyone will participate in the process.

A system that is holistic and includes departmental and individual performance planning, and ongoing coaching and evaluation

Tools that measure day-to-day work functions as well as activities that are project-based, challenging, and developmental

Tools that provide the opportunity for employee development, motivation, and recognition

Tools that specify the training and resources employees will need in order to effectively and efficiently accomplish their job requirements and activities

A system—not a one-time process—that is continuous and which develops a climate that supports people working together to accomplish mutually agreed-upon activities

A system and tools that link individual performance activities to your library's strategic plan

If you are required to use a performance management plan or performance appraisal tool as mandated by your city or county, you may be able to augment that tool by using the techniques and workforms in this chapter. A number of ideas will be provided that you may be able to use separately or in tandem with other required forms and tools. Some local performance management systems are quite rigid, in which case you may only be able to use these concepts to broaden your own thinking or as the basis for advocating the use of a more strategic process locally.

An effective performance management system is a vital human resources tool you can use to create and preserve the alignment between the library's strategic plan (or the identified sense of where it wants to go) and the activities of front-line staff. Effective performance management systems include the following elements:

Strategic planning. The strategic planning process, as mentioned earlier, drives the entire performance management process. If your library doesn't have a strategic plan, you may have identified goals and objectives in a less formal way or determined annual priorities for units or departments. The important thing to remember is that this book is designed to help you identify and allocate the staff resources required to *implement* your service priorities. It is not designed to help you set those priorities. It will be very difficult to allocate staff resources effectively in the absence of clearly defined priorities. As the Cheshire Cat said to Alice, if you don't care where you're going, then it doesn't matter which way you go.

Departmental performance planning. Your strategic plan provides a direct link from your library's goals to the activities and work plans (usually annual) for each department or work unit in the library.

Individual performance planning. This occurs at the beginning of each yearly performance period and links each employee's performance to the department or unit's activities (which may have been articulated in an annual work plan)

and the overall strategic plan. The planning portion of the process is used to communicate and align employee and organizational expectations, as well as to gain the employee's commitment and buy-in to achieving the agreed-upon activities. Performance planning provides a clear understanding of the individual employee's performance activities and expectations while also promoting supervisor-employee communication. Employees and supervisors should agree on the activities and discuss time lines and other measures that will indicate success.

Training and resources. Effective performance management ensures that the necessary resources and support for achievement of goals are available.

Monitoring and coaching. Coaching should happen continuously throughout the year. Evaluation is ongoing, but is typically formalized only once or twice a year. Good coaching will give both employees and managers great comfort in providing positive as well as negative feedback as events happen, rather than waiting until the end of the year. Some systems include prescribed or mandatory check-ins (biannually or even quarterly) in addition to more informal, ongoing coaching, which could occur on a near-daily basis. These check-ins could be written into the evaluation form and would require that the employee and supervisor sign to indicate that a performance discussion has occurred. If you think your culture will be slow in adapting to coaching, this may be a good way to begin showing how beneficial two-way feedback can be. Of course, the predetermined check-ins should not be the only time supervisors and employees talk, but rather just a way of making sure it happens at least occasionally.

Evaluation. The formalized performance evaluation completes and restarts the cycle as employees and supervisors discuss the year's performance and the coming year's goals, challenges, and priorities. A successful evaluation cycle will provide greater consistency in your library rating system, as well as a shared understanding of what those ratings mean.

Each library's performance management system will have different program components based on that library's unique, individual needs and the requirements of its parent jurisdiction. One library might have a simple rating or evaluation system, while another might have a multipart performance-planning process involving a very deliberate series of training, coaching, mentoring, individual and work unit planning, formal and informal evaluation, and individual development planning pieces.

If your library doesn't have a performance management system in place, then you will want to consider these elements, your library's capacity to develop them, and clarify what you want to accomplish with a performance management system. Use staff focus groups, surveys, interviews, observation, and feedback from managers and staff members to determine why a performance management system is needed. Are employees asking what the library's top priorities are? Do they want to know or need clarification about what's expected of them and how well they're doing? Are managers asking for greater accountability? Is everyone on the staff clear as to how their work helps the library accomplish its goals? Is assigned work done satisfactorily, completely, and on time or is there confusion about work assignments and completion timetables? Do managers and employees feel that exceptional work is recognized and inferior work is corrected? Are staff development and training needs recognized and addressed? A well-designed performance management system can provide a way to respond to each of these questions. Use the forms and procedures provided in this chapter to build your own system if one isn't already in place.

If you decide to build your own performance management system, it will be very important for you to review the recommendations in the "Planning to Plan" section of chapter 1. Performance management is a subject that affects every staff member, and they will all be interested in the process. You will want to decide which staff to involve in the process and you will need to identify the responsibilities of everyone involved. You will probably want to develop a list of the tasks and steps required to create your performance management system, and you will certainly want to identify the approval points within those tasks and steps. Finally, you will need to develop a plan to ensure that all staff are kept informed throughout the process and that staff have opportunities for input at appropriate times.

Step 4.2
Manage and Monitor a Performance Management System

You may have a clearly defined and perfectly planned performance management system, but you won't receive any benefits from that system unless it is effectively managed and monitored. There are few things more detrimental to staff morale than to have some supervisors who follow the performance management process carefully and other supervisors who ignore, or worse, subvert the process.

Performance Management System Training

No component of implementing a performance management system is more important than ensuring that everyone in the library is educated about the elements of your library's system and understands how to implement it—and this is equally true if you are using a system mandated by your funding body or using a system you developed internally. Employees need to understand more than how to complete the forms. They need to know how the system was developed, who provided input, and what it means to them as employees. Any time you change a performance management system there are questions about compensation and rewards. Staff will want to know if their pay will be linked to performance. Will an outstanding rating result in an increase in pay? If so, how much? Will a poor rating mean they are immediately fired? Will it mean they lose a step increase? Will the employee need to go through a work improvement program?

Your training should include specific evaluator modules so that supervisors and managers can be trained in objectively rating employees and provided with assistance in developing, giving, and receiving coaching feedback, in avoiding rating errors, and so on. Training, communication, and education options can include open sessions for employees, departmental meetings with the department head and supervisors, brown-bag lunch sessions for employees to ask questions, and so on.

Figure 23 provides one possible outline that could be used to develop training for your supervisors and managers on your performance management system.

FIGURE 23
Suggested Training Outline

- ✓ Basics of performance management—what is it?
- ✓ How system was developed (if new)
- ✓ How feedback from staff was incorporated (if applicable)
- ✓ Characteristics of the system
- ✓ Performance management model and performance evaluation process (description of the components and tools)
- ✓ How individual and department activities flow from strategic plan
- ✓ How to develop individual work plan for performance year
- ✓ Description of two basic types of activities (basic and development)
- ✓ How to write SMART activities
- ✓ Description of performance essentials (if applicable)
- ✓ Coaching
- ✓ Giving/receiving feedback
- ✓ Separate employee and manager training packages
- ✓ Communications skills
- ✓ How to prepare for and conduct a performance review meeting
- ✓ Documentation
- ✓ Performance rating errors

If yours is a library system where all performance evaluations are completed at the same time, then your training should be tied to that cycle. A full training session should be offered at the rollout of the program and six to eight weeks before evaluations are due. Three to six hours should be allocated to training supervisors. The session should be interactive and include an opportunity for all to try out their skills, learning, and behaviors. Build short cases, examples, and role plays into the training. Let participants try out providing feedback to an employee and obtain feedback from their peers on the content and process. Do the same with rating errors. Create model cases and see how the participants in the training session would evaluate the library's mock employee. Is there consistency? Are there errors?

A brief training, perhaps as one or a series of brown-bag lunches, should be provided two to four months later. Targeting these sessions to specific topics, such as coaching, providing constructive feedback, evaluating fairly and consistently, what to do when an employee adamantly disagrees, and so on, is worthwhile.

Nonsupervisory employees should receive training, education, or at least an orientation to the performance management process as well. It does not have to be as extensive as the supervisory training, but it should cover the basics so employees can be partners in and understand the process and their role in it. After all, every employee will be an evaluator or evaluatee and many will be both.

Monitoring Implementation

You cannot assume that because all supervisors are fully trained to implement the library's performance management system, they are all going to do so in exactly the same way. Performance management can be a difficult process for some supervisors, particularly those in small units that have a long-term, close-knit staff. The emotional ties that develop between supervisors and employees in situations like that can make objective evaluation difficult, and these supervisors tend to avoid the whole subject if possible. On the other hand, occasionally a supervisor uses the performance management process to threaten or intimidate staff.

Managers throughout the organization should carefully monitor the performance management activities of supervisors who report to them in order to ensure consistent and equitable application of the process.

Step 4.3
Develop Individual Performance Plans

Each employee needs to know what she is supposed to do, how well she is supposed to do it and what that success will look like, and how her duties and responsibilities fit into the big picture of the library. This is the time to capitalize on the work you did in chapter 2. You've identified most of the activities that employees need to undertake in order to meet the goals of the library's strategic service plan. Now you build on this earlier work and use the activities as the basis for an individual performance plan. This plan lists the activities each employee will perform over the course of the year in order to fulfill assigned goals linking to the library's service priorities. The plan also lists the time frame for accomplishing each activity, the measures of success for it, and any resources that will be needed. Workform 8, Individual Performance Plan, can be used to plan individual activities for the performance period. The workform should be completed initially by the employee, then reviewed with the supervisor. Supervisors should provide support to employees in completing the workform, particularly if they are new or recently promoted to their position. The detailed recommendations for writing performance activities provided below should be carefully reviewed by both employees and supervisors. Coming to agreement on appropriate performance activities will be an iterative process between the employee and supervisor.

Writing Measurable Performance Activities

Performance expectations should be measurable and based on observable job performance behaviors. As such, these expectations are in actuality performance activities. These describe the specific tasks an employee will carry out to achieve the library's goals and objectives. Activities, as noted earlier, result in an output of things done or services delivered. They form the basis for an individual performance plan because they explicitly define the work that an employee is expected to do.

An effective method for writing measurable performance expectations/performance activities is to use the SMART mnemonic:

> *Specific.* Detail what needs to be done. Make sure it is not vague or open to interpretation.

Measurable. Make the performance activity easy to measure by providing numbers, amount of change, percentage of change, and so on.

Achievable. The activity should be a stretch, but achievable. Use action verbs like *create, build, lead, develop,* and so on.

Relevant. Relate the individual activity to the departmental activities.

Time-sensitive. Indicate how long the activity will take or when it will be completed.

Writing SMART activity statements is not hard, but it does require some careful thinking. The following is an example of a series of SMART activities compared to those that are vague and not measurable.

Vague	SMART
Present programs in the community.	Conduct 12 storytimes at nonlibrary locations such as day care centers.
Prepare for Summer Reading Program.	Have all Summer Reading Materials ready to go to the printer by XX [date] and available for distribution no later than XX [date].
Manage the adult literature and history collections.	Weed a minimum of 5 percent of the 800 collection by XX [date].
Evaluate customer satisfaction.	Design and implement a Materials Availability Survey by the end of the first quarter. Review the data from the Materials Availability study, and by XX [date] develop an action plan to improve the percentage of people who indicated satisfaction with the library's collection.

The differences between the two sides of the table are obvious. An employee presented with or suggesting the performance activities on the left side would not have a clear idea of exactly what is expected, when it is expected, and so on. And yet how many of us have seen or even written these types of vague and abstract activities for employees and expected them to hit the ground running? Instead, activities must indicate the end result and describe it in SMART terms; for example, by

quantity: make four community contacts each quarter

quality: that receive a rating of 4 or more out of 5

time frame: by the fifth of each month

percentages or other specific measures: respond to 90 percent of reference questions the same day

cost or budget: cost per item, or overtime expenses incurred

When writing SMART activities, think about the breadth or depth of each activity, its complexity, intensity of effort, and the time it may take for completion. Don't forget to consider the volume of work that will be necessary to create the desired outcome, who else is involved, how the work will facilitate or hinder responsiveness to library and customer needs, how the work will foster or hinder positive relationships among staff and library customers, the quality of the work that is expected, and how the activity is linked to the strategic plan.

When thinking about the quality of the work, remember that quality does not have to be an abstract concept with nebulous or no measures. Quality can be increased and measured by identifying, reducing, or eliminating errors and mistakes, complaints, do-overs, waste, unnecessary complexity, and the time required to do the job, and by reducing the number, difficulty, and length of time of each of the action steps required to do the activity (especially when project-based or where there are interdependencies that must be accounted for). You could measure the number of customer complaints, calculate findings of satisfaction or dissatisfaction from customer surveys, or measure accuracy (books shelved, accounts paid, materials cataloged, employees paid the right amount of money, etc.).

Some performance activities lend themselves better to measures related to quantity or volume of work. With some activities, quantity can be measured by setting standards for the number of "work units" to be completed, for instance, phone calls to be made, books processed, shelved, or cataloged, puppet shows developed, new teen programs created, ILL requests filled, school visits completed, and so on. These types of measures may work well for jobs in the processing, circulation, or shipping/receiving departments, but not nearly as well for reference librarians or administrative assistants.

Now that you have a picture of how to write SMART activity statements that are specific, measurable, achievable, relevant, and time-sensitive, you are ready to write individual performance activities. As you write your activities, reflect upon the following questions:

> Does the activity support the library's goals?
>
> Is it results-oriented?
>
> Is it supported by the needed authority and resources?
>
> Is it challenging? Reasonable? Attainable? Measurable?
>
> Can it be exceeded?
>
> Is it expressed in specific versus general terms?
>
> Is the activity agreed upon between the employee and the supervisor?
>
> Is it SMART?!

With the answers to these questions, you are ready to plan the training and tools that employees need to successfully complete their performance activities.

In addition, for performance planning purposes, there are two categories of activities: the activities that represent an employee's day-to-day work and relate back to the library's goals and objectives (or relate to work that is in support of those goals), and personal or professional development activities. Personal or professional development activities are those that improve the employee's ability to perform a job function or prepare her for another job or broader responsibilities.

Generally, the day-to-day activities relate back to the goals and objectives in the strategic plan. For example, one of the goals in the Tree County Library plan is, "Children and teens will have the resources they need to complete their school assignments and succeed in school." One of the objectives designed to measure whether or not the goal is accomplished is, "Each year, all fourth-grade classes in the county will visit the library." There is a clear link between this goal and its objective and the activity of preparing for and presenting class tours. You can see that a number of other activities would also connect to this goal: making school visits, preparing information to distribute to schools inviting them to the library for a tour, issuing library cards and checking out library materials during the school tour, helping the students find desired materials, and so on.

Personal or professional development activities relate back to the knowledge, skills, and abilities of the job (see chapter 2 for a discussion of KSAs). A public service librarian who will be managing a grant-funded program might take a course on project management or an advanced course in using Microsoft Excel, if those are skills she hasn't yet acquired.

The number of activities in each category will vary from year to year depending on the library's needs and priorities and the employee's career and personal aspirations. In general, you will find that for employees in jobs that are more routine, especially where the employee is tenured in the job, the performance plan will be focused on basic, everyday activities. Even so, at least one developmental activity should be agreed upon by both the employee and supervisor for the performance period. Working with the employee to identify a developmental activity underscores the value the library places on continual learning and growth. An experienced circulation clerk may be very familiar with circulation functions and perform them flawlessly, but she may decide to take a class in basic Spanish so she can more easily and comfortably converse with the library's new customers. A seasoned delivery driver may be encouraged to take the county's new defensive driving course or a course on lifting correctly to prevent back injuries.

Discussing and agreeing on activities during the annual performance planning session ensure that employees and supervisors have the same priorities and expectations for the job in the coming year and that the employee has the needed time, training, resources, authority, staff, and learning opportunities to be successful.

Providing Needed Training and Tools

Once the SMART basic and developmental activities have been agreed to, there is one more step to take. This step is too often neglected and may take some thought, but it is well worth your while. Neglecting this step often results in poor performance, disappointing results, or failed or delayed projects. It involves stepping back and reflecting on the question: Does this employee have the training, tools, time, staff, authority, and resources to accomplish the activities in the performance plan? Does she have the time and resources to do all of them?

In the rush of excitement and desire to undertake projects, we often forget to ask: "Can I do this?" or "Can this employee do it?" The following are real work scenarios with examples of the questions that need to be asked and the issues to be pondered prior to committing to an activity in a performance planning session.

> If an employee is going to move from behind the circulation desk to driving the bookmobile, does she have the appropriate driver's license? What is involved in getting that license? Will it take time? Money? Who will pay for it?

> If a librarian is going to assume the task of chairing a committee to plan services to teens, her excitement about the project will not be sufficient to ensure a smooth process if she hasn't learned about team roles or completed facilitation or meeting-management training.

The cataloging manager recently promoted to head technical services may not have sufficient time this year to serve on the collection development committee or undertake special projects.

Does the branch manager who is opening the new mini-branch in the mall have sufficient staff to run it during hours that parallel the mall's schedule? Are the resources available to provide services in a branch that is required to be open each and every hour the mall is open to the public?

Does the librarian who is now going to assume responsibilities for the new birth-to-two-year-old program know about emergent literacy theory and practice? Does she know the music and stories for this population? Has she conducted a lap-sit storytime since her own teenager was a baby? Would taking a class, reading some books, or being mentored by a colleague help her facilitate the success of the birth-to-two program?

Is the library associate tasked with developing a new customer survey statistically savvy? Will she need to learn SPSS (Statistical Package for the Social Sciences)? Should she hire a consultant? Should she work with a faculty member at the local college or university? Does the library have the necessary software?

Does the employee's authority match the level of responsibility given to her? Employees must be given the authority to accomplish each activity. This authority should be made transparent to others via, for example, a team charter and public announcement of a committee chairmanship.

Training is critical to ensuring that employees are doing the right work efficiently and effectively in order to achieve their performance activities. Training can also help move the library toward better employee retention

While some training will require paying for instruction, there are a number of ways to develop staff skills and abilities that do not cost money or require a consultant. Mentoring programs, job rotation, and task force assignments take some committee time to develop, but they will not cost the library additional money. Nor do they require implementation by an HR person. Your library staff, perhaps working as a task force (another development opportunity), can help to create a staff development plan. The plan might include some of the following components:

Training and development programs put on and sponsored by your local government

Partnerships with your local college or university

IMLS/LSTA-funded development plans

Pooling resources with other public libraries and your state library association

Researching best practices on mentoring

Creating a format for individual development plans or 360-degree feedback

Forming a study group

Planning to learn something new as a staff together; for example, Spanish or a new software product

Creating a leadership academy

HOW WILL YOU PAY FOR TRAINING?

An early step is to check if there are available funds for the library and its staff in the city or county budget. You might be eligible to piggyback on training that is provided or brought in by the human resources department of your local parent jurisdiction. Some of this training is excellent, so it makes sense to at least find out what is available. Contact your local college and community college for additional possible partnerships. A public library system did this very successfully, using faculty to offer classes on-site that formed the basis of the library's leadership academy. Capitalize on your relationships with other local libraries and look for synergies. Share the expense of a costly speaker or consultant. See who will be speaking at your state library association conferences, and if it's someone you are interested in having at your library, invite her to your library before or after her engagement. It will save you travel costs and probably some fees as well. LSTA (Library Services and Technology Act) grants are often available to support training, and Library Friends groups and foundations are very generous in supporting training and development activities. As you can see, training is critical, and there is no excuse for ignoring this tool for productivity, effectiveness, and retention.

Ultimately it is everyone's responsibility to develop the library's workforce: the employee, her manager, and the board of trustees. The person who holds the major share of the responsibility, though, is the employee. Employees who do not develop will become obsolete very quickly, not only in the library world, but everywhere else as well. Employees should do the work to develop and advance themselves personally and professionally.

As you can see, considering whether or not the needed training and resources are available is a critical part of the planning process. Before coming to the final agreement on an employee's performance activities, make sure that the plan as a whole is realistic and achievable. This assessment will require the supervisor and employee to agree that the employee will have sufficient time, training, authority, and support to carry out the activities identified.

Completing Individual Performance Plans

The employee (possibly with her supervisor's help) should now be ready to complete Workform 8. She should have sufficient information to identify her activities and to describe them in SMART terms. After she has filled out the form, she and her supervisor should meet to discuss the activities, to be sure that these reflect the library's priorities and link to the library's overall goals and objectives. They should also discuss the training, resources, and support required to successfully carry out the identified activities, the time frames involved, and what successful accomplishments would look like. The supervisor may have to find needed resources. If an activity requires support from another branch, unit, or department, the employee or supervisor may need to coordinate the sharing of resources, especially staff. The process of meeting face-to-face to discuss and come to agreement on the activities of the individual performance plan is key to the library's successfully accomplishing its goals. The performance planning process and the personal meeting clarify what is expected of an employee, ensure that an individual's work activities are congruent with the library's organizational goals, and provide an opportunity for the employee and her immediate supervisor to discuss and refine work priorities and the components necessary (such as training and other organizational support) for successful work performance.

Step 4.4
Monitor and Coach Individuals

Library employees need to know what's expected of them and how their activities fit into the overall strategic direction the library is taking. But knowing isn't enough. They need ongoing feedback and support. The overall purpose of a performance management system is to help employees achieve their highest potential as they make their contributions to the library's strategic goals.

Well-designed and written activity statements will focus employees on results, not just doing things. These activity statements can both measure and motivate. People like to succeed. Challenging but doable activities energize employees, and measures of success help them see where their efforts are paying off and where adjustments should be made. Of course, feedback (especially positive) is critical. Checking on employees' progress lets them know priorities and also lets them report how they are doing, where they are doing well, and where they may need help.

Monitoring involves keeping track of what's been agreed to and checking in to see that it has been done. To do this you must identify the data needed to monitor the activities that employees are carrying out, develop a plan to collect and record that data, and then develop a way to review the data. If problems occur, employees need to understand that they have a responsibility to let their supervisors know so that the problem or issue can be addressed and resolved. Many of the statistics you routinely collect can be the basis for much of the monitoring you'll need to do. Unfortunately, many libraries collect statistics and other forms of data but never really do much with them except fill out the state library report at the end of the year.

If all branch managers who work for the Tree County Library are supposed to make four community contacts each quarter, the information on the contacts made should be kept and reported. If a particular branch manager is showing, through her reporting, that she has not made these contacts, then the reasons why should be identified and discussed. If no one collects and reports the data and if nothing is done if the contacts aren't made, then this activity has become meaningless. It was selected originally because it was deemed an important activity, crucial to the library's accomplishing its goals. It shouldn't be allowed to slip. The branch manager's manager needs to address the issue, which takes us to the next phase of the performance cycle: coaching.

A critical and continuous part of the performance cycle is coaching. Coaching is a day-to-day event and involves observing employees as they work, providing them with feedback (both positive and negative), reinforcing the feedback by being consistent in both positive and negative comments, and giving and asking for feedback as a supervisor or manager. As previously mentioned, coaching can also occur at more formalized events such as quarterly or six-month progress review meetings. Employees need to know on an ongoing basis how they are doing throughout the year. They should never be surprised by what they hear at the formal, annual performance review meeting.

When coaching, managers provide instruction, direction, guidance, encouragement, and correction as the employee works on the activities for which she is responsible. Coaching should be part of the daily work routine and should provide a learning opportunity for employees as well as recognition for a job well done.

Offering feedback requires preparation of both content and the manner in which it will be given. Guidelines for both giving and receiving feedback are provided in figure 24.

FIGURE 24
Guidelines for Giving and Receiving Feedback

Guidelines for Giving	Guidelines for Receiving
• Recognize both positive and "challenging" areas of performance.	• Listen carefully and actively
• Identify the issue or topic you wish to discuss	• Don't be defensive or overreact
• Be specific about what happened	• Paraphrase to ensure understanding
• Be direct; get to the point	• Use clarifying questions
• Be sincere and do not give mixed messages	• Ask for actual examples of the behavior being discussed vs. a nonspecific statement like "I don't like how you acted"
• If giving positive feedback, be appreciative	• Identify trouble spots and resolve how to avoid them in the future
• If giving negative feedback, express concern	• Ask how it could be done better
• Give feedback face-to-face, as soon as possible (positive) or as soon as appropriate (negative)	• Ask for more feedback
• State observations of what you saw, not your analysis or opinion	
• Listen	

Just as important as knowing when and how to give feedback is knowing when not to give feedback. Feedback shouldn't be given if you don't know enough about the circumstances of the behavior; if it is about something the person has little or no power to change; if it is a low self-esteem day for you or the employee; or if your purpose is not really to promote improvement but to put someone on the spot (a "gotcha"). The time and place need to be appropriate as well, and unless the feedback is positive, it should not be given in the presence of customers or other staff. Summarize the session when it is complete. Taking notes to prepare in advance is also helpful, to increase the likelihood of covering every point you want to make without getting off track or forgetting an important example.

Receiving feedback can be difficult. In a library that provides constructive feedback rather than burying problems or hoping they will just go away or fix themselves, employees at all levels will find themselves to be recipients of feedback. Paying attention to the guidelines will make receiving feedback a learning experience rather than a threat.

A coaching discussion with an employee regarding an area of work performance that needs improvement should involve asking questions to gather relevant details about the issue; identifying, discussing, and selecting an approach to address the issue; agreeing on the desired outcome; and setting a follow-up date to review and check on progress on that specific issue. The follow-up is very important. In a performance-based culture, the employee must take accountability for performance improvement or new skills acquisition, and supervisors can help by providing feedback and support and expressing confidence in the employee's ability to accomplish the outcome effectively.

Work to reinforce an employee's self-esteem when providing feedback by focusing on the work, not the person. Be specific and sincere. For example, saying, "I appreciate the extra time you spent editing the report. There were no typos or errors. I enjoyed reading it. Thanks!" is much more meaningful to an employee than, "Good job, Susie." When people feel good about themselves they are more motivated, productive, and cooperative. And when they know exactly what it was they did that you thought was an example of excellent performance, they will be able to replicate it. This type of feedback, recognizing the employee's strengths and accomplishments, helps build self-assurance, which is a powerful correlate to high performance.

Finally, make sure that employees are allowed and even encouraged to ask their supervisor for feedback. A two-way communication process is thereby established and employees aren't sitting around waiting for feedback—positive or negative. In addition, if a supervisor isn't "taking to" the coaching idea, empowering employees to ask for feedback may encourage the supervisor to feel more comfortable with the process, and it certainly gives employees some accountability by being active participants in the coaching and feedback loop.

Step 4.5
Evaluate and Rate Individuals

Performance management should be an ongoing and continuous process. However, there is always a formal evaluation at the end of each performance cycle. Many libraries are required to use evaluation forms provided by the local government. If you have the option of developing your own evaluation forms, consider using Workform 9, Performance Evaluation Tool, as your template. Workform 9 is a review of the information on Workform 8 and is expanded to cover your library's "performance essentials." Performance essentials are the behaviors, skills, attributes, performance factors, and proficiencies that every library employee is expected to possess and display. They are limited in number to allow you to focus on them and are critical to the library's success.

Four common, useful performance essentials are proposed: job knowledge, quality/productivity, customer service, and (if applicable) managerial effectiveness. The definitions of these essentials are provided on Workform 9. At the beginning of the evaluation period, the employee and supervisor should review the performance essentials and establish measures so both agree on what success "looks like" in behavioral terms. Generally libraries, working with a committee, select and define their own performance essentials based on the values and direction of the library.

Supervisors and managers should be prepared for each performance evaluation meeting. Remember, although the supervisor may have fifteen reviews to conduct, this one is most important to this employee. Supervisors should review the employee's activities and her actual performance. The self-evaluation, if used, should be submitted to the supervisor in advance so that she may review it prior to the evaluation meeting. There should be no surprises at this point, since you've been reviewing and coaching throughout the year, but it does not hurt to re-familiarize yourself with this information at this point. Anticipate the employee's potential objections to a less than stellar rating and think about responses, even rehearsing dialogue. Of course, you will also want to have prepared some activities to discuss for the next performance cycle.

Figure 25 provides guidelines for preparation of the person conducting the performance evaluation.

When rating employees, be sure to go back over coaching notes and other documentation you may have. Think about the individual pieces of the performance picture. Did the employee successfully accomplish the day-to-day duties and responsibilities of the job description? Did the employee achieve each activity fully, as expected, on time and within budget (if those were parameters)? Remember, library priorities can easily have

---

FIGURE 25
Guidelines for Preparing and Conducting Performance Evaluations

Pre-interview

The evaluator should:

1. Be familiar with the review form, strategic plan, and instructions.

2. Understand the employee's job and responsibilities—review job description; critical knowledge, skills, abilities, and competencies; your notes over the course of the year; and other documentation relating to the employee's performance.

3. Consider the entire period to be evaluated, and not be influenced by out-of-the ordinary occurrences, good or bad. Think in terms of job requirements and the employee's performance throughout the performance period.

4. Strive to be objective and fair.

5. Use a positive approach; mention accomplishments and give practical and specific suggestions for improvement.

6. Do not use the performance review as a disciplinary tool.

7. Have specific examples to illustrate situations.

8. Plan what to say and how to say it.

9. Establish a draft of developmental activities.

10. Consult with your manager if there are questions or problems.

Time and place

1. Set up a meeting time that is at least two hours before the end of the employee's workday.

2. Avoid interruptions.

3. Set up a relaxed and unhurried meeting atmosphere.

4. Select a private place where conversations cannot be overheard.

5. Give the staff member sufficient time to review the evaluation prior to the review meeting.

Meeting

1. Set the employee at ease by getting her to talk about the job.

2. Go over each aspect of the employee's self-assessment.

3. Listen in an active way to the employee's remarks and views.

4. Emphasize employee's strengths and mention specific accomplishments.

5. Comment on improvements.

6. Be careful not to put the employee on the defensive.

7. Do not compare the employee with any other employees.

8. Evaluate the performance, not the person.

9. Make suggestions for improvements and ask for the employee's input.

10. Control the discussion tactfully.

11. Do not show anger.

12. Establish basic and development activities for the next evaluation period.

13. Ask if the employee wants to bring up any other points.

14. Avoid promises about salary increases, promotions, or transfers.

15. Summarize the key points of discussion and the plans of action agreed upon. This assures joint understanding and establishes expectations.

shifted during the year, and the employee's activities may have changed as well. Figure 26 provides some general definitions of three levels of performance: outstanding, fully successful, and needs improvement. The supervisor selects one of these rating levels for each activity and performance essential and writes comments to support the rating. Provide comments and examples of employees' performance, using facts, not your conclusions, opinions, or guesses about motivation.

As you can see from the sequence of performance management tasks, the system is designed to make very clear the connection between an employee's work (the activities she carries out) and the library's goals; to provide necessary monitoring, ongoing feedback, and monitoring; and to provide regular, formal evaluations or appraisals. For the system to be embraced by managers and employees alike, it is these positive aspects that

---

FIGURE 26
Performance Levels

Although it is recognized that an employee's overall job performance is made up of many factors, in general, performance may best be described as having the characteristics of one of the following levels.

Outstanding *Constantly Surpasses Expectations*	Fully Successful *Fully Achieves Expectations*	Needs Improvement *Needs Improvement to Achieve Expectations*
Performance constantly surpasses established expectations, requirements, or standards.	Performance consistently meets established expectations, requirements, or standards.	Performance does not fully meet established expectations, requirements, or standards.
Customarily increases job knowledge/skills to accomplish objectives. Regularly accepts and achieves noteworthy success on additional responsibilities.	Effectively applies and pursues opportunities to increase job knowledge/skills to complete objectives.	May not pursue developmental opportunities, improve performance, and/or apply new skills to meet standards.
Anticipates and proactively responds to changing situations and additional work assignments.	Readily adjusts to changing situations and additional work assignments.	Exhibits difficulty adjusting to changing situations or work assignments.
Contributes significantly to the organization's success well beyond job requirements.	Demonstrates proactive problem-solving to improve and/or adjust work processes.	May not exhibit proactive problem-solving to improve and/or adjust work processes.
Routinely seeks, accepts, and achieves extraordinary success on additional responsibilities.	Produces results dependably, on time, and accurately.	Performs inconsistently, possibly leading to some inaccurate, untimely, and/or undependable results.
Contributes and leads innovative, workable solutions to projects and/or problems. Accomplishes high work quality and productivity while dealing with obstacles to success.	Effectively meets the needs of customer-service relationships. Exhibits expected workplace courtesy and respect. Behavior positively influences working relationships.	At times, displays actions which are detrimental to customer-service relationships. May behave in a manner which is detrimental to the work group.
Demonstrates constant commitment to continuous improvement to increase job knowledge, customer service, and productivity.	Displays regular attendance to meet organizational needs. Often demonstrates flexibility to meet organizational needs.	May display irregular attendance that impacts work flow and organizational needs.

must be emphasized and supported. But there may be employees who do not, or are not able to, carry out agreed-upon activities satisfactorily and whose ratings on performance essentials indicate a need to improve in one or more areas. Guidelines for managing performance should acknowledge this possibility and require that a performance improvement plan be designed, with frequent check-in points as a way to assist the employee in improving her work performance.

While not appropriate as the beginning point of a disciplinary or termination process (the formal evaluation should not be the first time an employee is informed that her work is deficient), the performance evaluation and other documentation of substandard job performance should be used to substantiate or defend against disciplinary procedures.

It is critical that substandard work performance be carefully documented and the employee provided with a fair opportunity to correct identified deficiencies before discipline is imposed. A thorough coaching process can ensure that the employee does have the time and opportunity to adjust and improve the identified areas. In some instances, performance may improve, in others not, but the employee has been provided with the opportunity to address it. She will ultimately be accountable for whether or not improvements are made, provided the feedback is specific, within reach, and fair. For this reason, it's vital that managers not shy away from the important but sometimes time-consuming and detail-ridden process of coaching, monitoring, providing feedback, and recognizing improved performance. Ultimately, an employee who cannot effectively contribute to the success of the library is a detriment to the organization and her coworkers, who must carry the slack her inabilities create.

Employees should be proactive in this process and prepare for the evaluation as well. They should start two weeks before the performance evaluation meeting by reflecting on the year or performance period and taking notes of their responses to the questions posed in Workform 10, Self-Evaluation. This workform provides suggestions for helping employees think through their past year's performance, reflecting on strengths and areas that need development, and planning for the upcoming performance period. Employees should give the completed self-evaluation to their supervisor prior to the annual performance review meeting.

Consider giving the written draft evaluation to the employee prior to the meeting. Some libraries have found this to be a critical part of having a successful conversation about performance. Receiving the written evaluation ahead of time gives the employee an opportunity to reflect prior to the meeting. If this is done, it must be made clear to the employee that confidentiality is expected and that the evaluation process is not over until the employee and her supervisor have had a chance to discuss the draft and the employee's self-evaluation (if done) in the performance review meeting.

After both the employee and supervisor have prepared, it is time to hold the performance review meeting. Sufficient quiet, uninterrupted time should be allocated for it. The purpose of the performance review meeting is to discuss and finalize the performance evaluation. Agenda items should include reviewing the job description requirements, individual performance plan, and ratings for the year's work activities. Start with an employee self-appraisal. How does the employee think she's done? In this situation, the employee is doing the talking and the supervisor is doing most of the listening. Identify any potential differences, discuss discrepancies with the employee, and ask the employee to lead the discussion about the problem area. Supervisors should ask for the employee's reactions and discuss the reasons for successes and the causes of problems. They should then review the overall performance rating and ask the employee for ideas for continuous improvement. Try to conduct a problem-solving discussion, reach agreement on performance problems, and together establish a development plan for moving forward.

The table below provides a few examples of how to provide specific feedback during the performance review meeting. The column on the left is compared to the nonspecific wording on the right. As you can see, the feedback on the left provides the employee with much more information about what work behaviors are considered to be good performance.

Specific Feedback	**Nonspecific Feedback**
Customers called me on five occasions because Bill hadn't gotten back to them with information they needed.	Bill is too lazy to provide good service to customers. (judgment, not fact)
Suzy noticed that our copier broke down frequently, and she brought me the brochure for a different brand, which she used at her last job.	Suzy shows initiative. (not a specific example)
As a member of the work team to implement the new self-check system, Mary Anne invited others to express their views. One member was reluctant to speak, so Mary Anne talked to her privately.	Mary Anne listens to and considers all points of view.

Be sure to reinforce good performance when an employee uses skills or behaviors well, especially as a follow-up to coaching done throughout the year. Reinforce good behaviors, even if the desired outcome was not achieved. Don't reinforce undesirable actions or skills. Above all, be specific, timely, and sincere.

Performance Rating Errors

There are many performance rating errors that managers need to be aware of and avoid, including the following ones.

Past influence. Something the employee did (negative or positive) eight months ago influences your rating of the entire year's events.

Recent events. A good or bad event of the past month is allowed to outweigh or overshadow events of the entire year.

Compatible ("similar to me"). People relate better to, and may be inclined to rate higher, people they feel are "like them" and with whom they identify.

Few observations. Too little data can prevent you from forming an objective assessment of the year.

Generalizations. "Oh, all of those circulation clerks did a fine job this year. I'll give them all the same rating." Maybe so, but maybe not. Don't lump people together.

Historical. The employee has always received high ratings in the past, so even though her work has been slipping lately, the evaluator is reluctant to reduce the rating because "she's always been such a good worker."

Potential equals performance. An individual's potential, in your opinion, may far outweigh their actual performance. Rate on actual performance only.

Personality conflicts. You don't necessarily have to want to spend time socially with someone to give them a high rating. Ratings are based on an individual's performance, not their ability, or desire, to be your friend.

You should certainly avoid rating errors based on biases related to race, gender, age, nationality, or sexual orientation. Likewise, don't be swayed into giving high ratings to those who merely look busy or "stay late" with no apparent increase in the quantity or quality of work.

Step 4.6
Plan for the Next Cycle

The performance management process described by Steps 4.1–4.5 is typically completed each year in a library. Although you will not want to revise or substantively change your performance management process (Step 4.1) every year, you will probably want to review the process and discuss any problems with supervisors at the end of each annual cycle. You may be able to identify changes that you could make to streamline or strengthen parts of the process.

Training (Step 4.2) should be an annual event whether or not the performance management system has changed. Supervisors who have used the process can attend a short refresher course, but new supervisors should be required to attend the complete training program. Too often new supervisors are introduced to the performance management system in an informal way by a colleague or manager and, as a result, they often don't fully understand the system or their responsibilities.

Of course, each employee will develop a new individual performance plan each year (Step 4.3). That plan can be developed as a part of the employee evaluation and rating process (Step 4.5) or it can be a separate process that begins at the conclusion of the evaluation period. Monitoring and coaching employees (Step 4.4) are ongoing activities, and the evaluation of employees occurs annually on a cycle set by the library or by the library's governing authority.

Summary

Creating a performance management system is critical to your library's success in meeting its strategic objectives and community needs. This process moves libraries toward a performance-based culture where results count and all staff are accountable. The key points of this model are to create activities which directly support the library's strategic objectives; explicitly describe performance expectations collaboratively with the employee, coach the employee at appropriate points along the way of completing activities; reward successful behavior and accomplishments; discourage unsuccessful behaviors which hinder the employee from meeting the activities; and directly confront areas for improvement. Performance should be documented in a formal evaluation which is the culmination of observation and discussion with the employee. Feedback must be objective, specific, and address behaviors, not individual personalities.

As a final note, in some library systems, performance appraisals are completed for all employees at one time during the year (at the beginning or end of the fiscal year, for example). In other organizations the evaluation date coincides with the employee's anniversary date, meaning that evaluations are staggered throughout the year. Whichever case applies to your library, just be aware of the time involved in developing activities, holding the evaluation meetings, etc., so that employees and managers are allotted sufficient time to complete the formal evaluation process successfully rather than cramming it in because "it's that time of year and I've got to get these done."

Note

1. Sandra Nelson and June Garcia, *Creating Policies for Results: From Chaos to Clarity* (Chicago: American Library Association, 2003).

Chapter 6

High-Impact Retention: Retaining the Best and the Brightest

MILESTONES

By the time you finish this chapter you will be able to

- understand why employees want to stay employed in a library
- create and sustain a culture of positive employee relations
- accommodate generational differences when designing retention and development programs
- develop employees through formal and informal means
- build and maintain effective feedback and recognition systems
- confidentially solicit employees' opinions about their job satisfaction, needs, and wants

How can a library generate and maintain commitment among its employees? This has always been a challenging process and is becoming more difficult every year. Many of the people currently working in libraries have been employed by the same library for 5, 10, 15, or even 20 years. It is not uncommon to find that over 50 percent of the employees in a library have never worked elsewhere. However, the realities of library employment are changing rapidly, and these fresh challenges are quite different.

In this new world a person's education alone does not qualify her for a job. Instead, library managers are writing job descriptions that focus on a prospective employee's knowledge, skills, and abilities, and they may also define her needed competencies. (See chapter 3 for more information on job descriptions.)

Library jobs are no longer immutable. The work is continually evolving and the way the work is managed is also changing. The old bureaucratic and hierarchical structure is being modified and replaced with one that is flat, networked, and nimble. More libraries are moving toward cross-functional and self-managed teams, with each team responsible for a range of tasks. Employees expect to be included in discussions about the library's future and want to have a voice in making important decisions.

Library staff are expected to continue to develop their KSAs while on the job and should be given opportunities to do so. In turn, their job tenure depends on their ability to perform. This continual growth and development makes the employee more valuable in her current and any future position in the library. Employees are expected to actively support the library's vision and values. When they can no longer do that, they are expected to look for new opportunities in other libraries, or other organizations.

These expectations reflect today's employment reality and may be very different from the expectations that staff brought to their jobs twenty or even five years ago. The psychological contract of a "job for life" has been broken. Public libraries twenty years from now will not be employing the person they hired last year or will hire next year. That person is likely to have had seven jobs by then—in three different careers! We are increasingly seeing an exchange of lifelong employment for "mutuality of purpose," where an employee can be expected to do a great job for an employer as long as she is provided with challenges, opportunities, and work/life balance.

Building and maintaining employee commitment is a process, one that begins during recruitment and ends after retirement. The key question, then, is how to go about this process of retaining the best and the brightest. The easiest place to start is with yourself. Think about your needs and wants. Ask yourself this question: What keeps me at my library? Think also about why your employees accept a job with your library and why they remain once they are hired.

There has been considerable research on this topic. Employees report that they stay with an employer for these reasons:

> They have a feeling of connection and know that they make a difference; they know how they and the work they do fits in and how they help the library accomplish its mission.
>
> They feel valued; their concerns, ideas, and suggestions are genuinely sought and listened to.
>
> They are respected and recognized for the work they do.
>
> There is a feeling of safety in the work environment.
>
> They have opportunities for personal and professional growth: formal education, workshops, on-the-job training, new assignments, job rotation, and attendance at conferences.
>
> The work environment promotes continuous learning: jobs that are designed to be interesting and stimulating, and the opportunity to participate on committees and task forces to create and implement improvements.
>
> There is good management as well as good communication with senior management. A bad supervisor is most often cited as the reason why employees leave an employer.
>
> There are fair pay and benefits. Even though many work in libraries because they love libraries and support their mission, employees have to receive pay

and benefits that allow them to live a comfortable life. While pay does not motivate an employee to stay, pay that is not fair, especially in relation to peers, is a demotivator.

Today's reality is that the library cannot afford a culture of entitlement, nor can it afford to lose employees who add value. The truth is that today your employees have choices as to where they work; they are not limited to the library in the community in which they live. It is incumbent on library leadership to create a culture that supports the retention of the right employees. Management training is key, as is knowing and responding to what employees want.

TASK 5: DEVELOP AND IMPLEMENT A RETENTION PLAN

Task 1: Assess Required Staff Resources
Task 2: Describe the Job
Task 3: Identify the Right Person for the Right Job
Task 4: Develop and Implement a Performance Management System
Task 5: Develop and Implement a Retention Plan
    Step 5.1: Plan the project
    Step 5.2: Understand workforce needs and expectations
    Step 5.3: Create the culture
    Step 5.4: Define expectations
    Step 5.5: Provide training
    Step 5.6: Build commitment

Using your own experiences as well as research, you can begin to develop and implement a retention plan that fits your library, its culture, and its employees. The plan starts with knowing the members of your library's workforce and engaging them to high performance and commitment.[1] It is also important to be cognizant of the political environment in which you work, as well as any civil service rules and union contracts that may affect the library's ability to "create the culture." Talk to your union representatives as well as local government HR staff. Get them on board with helping you make changes to your library's culture to the extent possible.

Step 5.1
Plan the Project

If you are going to complete this task, refer back to the "Planning to Plan" section of chapter 1. This information will help you plan the project, determine whether you need a committee, and if so, select committee members, create a charge, and formulate a communications plan.

Step 5.2
Understand Workforce Needs and Expectations

Earlier in this chapter, there was a discussion of how the expectations of employees and supervisors have changed. One of the key changes is the demise of the hierarchical "command and control" organizational structure in many libraries.[2] It is critical to train managers and supervisors to create and support a work environment that appreciates and fosters employee participation, encourages involvement in decision-making, and cultivates initiative and creativity. Even with training and development, a manager or supervisor who is familiar and comfortable with the more traditional bureaucratic management structure will not necessarily embrace this new approach or know how to make it work effectively. The work environment and employee culture desired by library leadership will not exist if those in middle management and supervisory positions are not also supportive of them.[3]

For this to happen, supervisors should be able to answer "yes" to each of these statements with regard to every person on their team:

1. I inquire about how to make work more satisfying for my employees.
2. I realize that I am mainly responsible for retaining the talent on my team.
3. I know my employees' career ambitions.
4. I take steps to ensure that my employees are continually challenged by their work.
5. I respect the work/life balance issues that my employees face.

Getting to know something about each person who works with you shows respect and concern and is highly correlated to retention. Employees want to know that you know who they are, that you've considered their needs as you make decisions, and that they have been heard.

Generational Diversity

There has been a lot of discussion about the differences between the various generations that work in libraries (or anywhere else) today. What follows is not meant to stereotype these generations, but rather to acknowledge some broad generalizations about their experience, behavior, expectations, and worldview. While each employee must be understood as an individual, understanding the four generational groupings—Traditionalists, Baby Boomers, Generation Xers (GenXers), and Millennials—can provide insight into factors that influence their approach to work and to the ability to manage and retain these employees in your library.[4]

Two approaches to understanding generational differences are referred to here. The first focuses on the events shaping the lives of each generational cohort, and thus shaping the culture, expectations, and worldview of its members. This is referred to as the Event Theory of Generations. The second approach is the Career Stage Theory, which states that the differences we perceive in the actions and behavior of the generations are attributed to their career stage, rather than to life events. Both viewpoints have implications for human resource management, policies, and practices. Both offer insights into the retention of employees at every age and career stage.

THE FOUR GENERATIONS AND EVENTS SHAPING THEIR LIVES

The four generations in the workplace today can be briefly characterized as follows.

Traditionalists. These employees were born before 1946. Traditionalists value hard work, dedication, and sacrifice. They respect rules and authority and they believe in duty before pleasure, self-sacrifice, and pulling oneself up by one's bootstraps. Loyalty to their employer, hard work, and honor are very important. The Great Depression, the New Deal, and World War II were the events that shaped the worldview of this generation.

Baby Boomers. Born between 1946 and 1964, many of these employees have come to librarianship as a second career. They tend to be more concerned with clarity of organizational structure, opportunities for growth and challenge, and rewards than Traditionalists, GenXers, or Millennials. Boomers seek stability, wear their values on their sleeves, possess a driven work ethic, value relationships, and often have a love/hate relationship with authority. They want to be involved, are competitive yet have a team orientation, and seek personal gratification and personal growth. They are optimistic and success-oriented. The worldview of the Boomers was shaped by the cold war, the civil rights movement, the Vietnam War and the antiwar movement, and the sexual revolution.

GenXers. Born between 1965 and 1981, these employees are results-oriented, value a work/life balance, are relatively unimpressed with authority, technologically literate, loyal to managers who treat them well, resourceful, self-reliant, pragmatic, independent, and are more mobile than stable in their job history. The members of this generation grew up in a time of reduced economic growth, and many of them were latchkey kids. Their worldview was influenced by Watergate, the women's liberation movement, the end of the cold war, and the first Gulf War. Some are described as "slackers" who do not live up to their potential, some as young people who work hard and play hard. Members of this generation have been characterized more by concern for individual growth and less with loyalty to their employer.

Millennials. Born between 1982 and 2000, these employees are collaborative, open-minded, achievement-oriented, confident, optimistic, inclusive, and technically savvy. They respect diversity, have high expectations, value public service, and are seen as more positive and more realistic than the GenXers.[5] Key events shaping their worldview were the rise of high technology and the Internet, growing up in a child-focused world, the terrorist attacks of September 11, 2001, and the second Gulf War. Many grew up in structured settings and value family and multiculturalism. This generation has also been referred to as GenY, the thumbers, the MySpace generation, and the 9/11s. Figure 27 provides additional insight into the differences among these groups.

Challenges among the four generations arise at the library because of each generation's differing attitude about work, the meaning of work, and the perceived value of the job being performed. There are seven areas of potential conflict: respect for authority, time on the job, advancement, recruiting and retention, skill building, work/life balance, and recognition.[6] While it is beyond the scope of this book to examine each in detail, a

FIGURE 27
Generational Differences

	Traditionalist Before 1946	Baby Boomer 1946–1964	GenXer 1965–1981	Millennial 1982–2000
Outlook	Practical	Optimistic	Skeptical	Hopeful
Work Ethic	Dedicated	Driven	Balanced	Ambitious
View of Authority	Respectful	Love/hate	Unimpressed	Relaxed, polite
Leadership by	Hierarchy	Consensus	Competence	Achievers
Relationships	Personal sacrifice	Personal gratification	Reluctant to commit	Loyal
Perspective	Civic	Team	Self	Civic

few potential conflict situations and tips on managing members of the four generations in the library follow.

The most significant differences exist between GenXers and members of the Baby Boom generation, first because the preponderance of most libraries' employees fall into one of these two groupings, and second, because the disparity between each group's life events and experiences is wide, thus creating the largest level of misunderstandings and tension.

Feedback is a major area of work/life clashes. Chapter 5 spoke of the importance of feedback in the performance management process, yet there are major differences between the generations in the content and style of feedback sought and given. Traditionalists tend to believe that "no news is good news" and are surprised, and sometimes bewildered, when their younger managers comment on their work. This is true of Boomers as well, who are accustomed to once-a-year feedback supported by lots of paperwork. In contrast, GenXers, and to a greater extent Millennials, expect feedback on a frequent basis. They also give immediate and honest feedback, which can be seen as pushy, arrogant, and inappropriate by others. GenXers need positive feedback and coaching to know they are on the right track. They will ask for it, and will sometimes interrupt to check for it. Millennials will ask as well. Many seek constant feedback, and in real time. They often interpret silence as their having done something wrong or as disapproval. They need to know how they are doing, right and wrong. Boomers often give but rarely receive feedback, and Traditionalists do not seek lavish praise, but they do appreciate acknowledgment of their efforts and accomplishments.

Authority is another area where differences in behavior are observed. Many Traditionalists and Boomers do not question the status quo or authority. This can cause confusion and resentment among GenXers and Millennials, who have been encouraged to challenge authority and make their voices heard. Boomer and Traditionalist managers too often view this challenge as a personal threat to them and their authority. These managers believe that they earned the right to make decisions and that their seniority and roles deserve respect. GenXers believe respect should be earned. Many Boomers managing GenXers feel challenged by this. At the same time, because their styles are different, too often GenXers and Millennials fail to listen actively to Boomers and Traditionalists, consequently losing the opportunity for gathering important information, perspective, mentoring, and guidance.

What can you do? If you are a Boomer or Traditionalist manager, go out of your way to engage, encourage, and capitalize on the KSAs, perspectives, and talents of the newer, younger members of your library. You will gain credibility and trust by developing and mentoring them. GenXers and Millennials need to acknowledge and respect Boomers' experience and abilities. GenXer staff should pursue learning opportunities and make managers aware of their willingness to take on new areas of responsibility, when ready. Millennials should seek mentors or coaches throughout the library, learn how to ask good questions, and listen patiently.[7]

TIPS FOR MANAGING MEMBERS OF EACH GENERATION

Traditionalists are at or near retirement age, but for a variety of reasons they may choose to continue working. They may be looking for a position that allows them to take advantage of the skills and networks they've developed over their working life, but with a schedule that gives them freedom to enjoy the activities they anticipate pursuing in retirement. If you are managing Traditionalist employees, be open to part-time employment and flexible working hours. Capitalize on their talents and institutional knowledge and provide them with the opportunity to coach and develop new talent. This is also critical for succession planning and to ensure a smooth transition of knowledge to the leaders of the future.

Some tips for managing a Boomer are to give her public recognition, provide her with opportunities to prove herself, show appreciation, let her know she has special contributions to make to the library, provide perks, acknowledge and reward her work ethic, explain the benefits of changes, and show respect for her experience and knowledge. Saying "I need you to do this for me" goes a long way to motivate a Boomer.

GenXers like challenges, new learning opportunities, specific feedback, flexible work options, and strong working relationships. GenXers like to do things their way; it's best to set the parameters of a project or activity and let them do the job their way. Don't micromanage, just coach and monitor progress. The work will be done. Include the members of this generation in decisions that are made and let them offer their ideas and opinions. GenXers want a mentor relationship with their boss, so finding the time for regular coaching and feedback is critical. To promote retention, remember that GenXers value a fun and informal work environment.

The members of the Millennial generation, the newest and fewest members of the library's workforce, are often compared to the Baby Boomers, who share a partiality for public service and volunteer activities. Many persons in this generational group thrive on learning opportunities and constant challenges. They want meaning in their job and often choose to work for organizations whose mission they value and for leaders who are honest and have integrity. You can best manage them with very regular feedback, flexible working options and schedules, and by acknowledging their ideas. Invite them to serve on committees and reinforce how the library, and their job, contribute to the community. Emphasize the meaningfulness of their role for the public and the services they provide to many people.

What else can you do? Think about the differences we've discussed as you consider the generations of employees working in the library. Talk about them with others. Ask yourself and others the following questions:

1. What were some defining historical events for each generation?
2. What was "cool" for each generation (movies, TV programs, music, toys, clothes, etc.)?
3. What are the core values of each generation?
4. Which generation predominates in the library?
5. What are the differences between members of the different generations who work at the library?
6. What is the best way to bring the generations together at work?
7. What advantages are there to having multiple generations working at the library?
8. Which generation do you admire the most at work and why?
9. What can each generation teach others?
10. What can each generation learn from others?

THE CAREER STAGE THEORY

An alternative approach is to analyze generational differences based on where each employee is in his or her career. From this perspective, one would expect 60-year-olds to be more interested in retirement policies and 20-year-olds to focus on vacation policies, regardless of the historical events and challenges faced by their generational cohort.

Career development generally means different things to newer, and often younger, employees interested in skill acquisition than it does to employees seeking management experience or pursuing an advanced degree. And for employees nearing retirement, mentoring or teaching opportunities may be the preferred form of career development. Supporting career development not only gives a library a means of aligning its goals with those of its workers, it also offers challenges to employees, which is a proven factor in building loyalty and retention.

Do not make assumptions about what employees at any point in their life cycle or career really want or need. To find out, be direct and ask them. Talk to employees frequently about their learning goals, their desire for personal and professional development, and their career at the library. This information should be captured in the employee's self-evaluation and discussed during the performance review meeting.

Career development is not a one-time process; it must be ongoing. It's about continuous learning and development and should not be viewed in the context of promotion alone. Especially in today's flatter organizational structures, there are fewer promotional opportunities, but many lateral opportunities offering challenges or new experiences. Most important, career development should be about both the individuals' needs and the library's needs. It's about linking and matching employee skills with the library's strategic priorities.

Step 5.3
Create the Culture

Why create, or change, a library's culture? The most important reason is to ensure that the library is able to attract and retain a committed workforce that is engaged and therefore gets the required work done in an effective and efficient way.

To ensure a committed workforce, the library needs to create the right intangibles—the culture—that not only attracts but also retains a talented workforce. It's not as hard as you think, but it is more time-consuming than you'd hoped! You start by understanding the workforce's needs and expectations. Then you work to align how you treat employees, to the fullest extent you can, with their needs (not yours, theirs) and your mission.

The term *workforce* refers to each and every one of your employees, from the young high school graduate in his first job to the veteran librarian with her thirty-year pin with the tiny emerald stone. Knowing what each employee wants and needs doesn't mean that you can give everyone what they want and need. It's about paying attention to each, "hearing" them, and doing what you can to support their needs, goals, and aspirations, all within a largely inflexible (public sector) framework. The challenge is to figure out ways to be more flexible.

Some of the ways to respond require little more than listening, hearing, and being creative. For example, it is important to keep in mind that different people define success differently. While one of your newest library school graduates might aspire to be the library director in a few short years, the other one who just joined your staff is defining her success in terms of work/life balance. She wants a traditional family. She exercises at the gym three mornings a week, does a lot of volunteer work during the week and on weekends (at the soup kitchen on Wednesday, and building a house with Habitat for Humanity on weekends), and plays soccer or volleyball at 5:30 p.m. twice a week.

And yet both of these Generation X librarians want to be continually learning and challenged. Both want to know the latest technology and trends. Both expect to be in on all decisions affecting their work and are committed to working in an organization that has meaning. It is important to create a culture that emphasizes

- participation
- shared decision-making
- sense of purpose and value
- initiative
- feedback
- creativity
- social aspects of the workplace
- balance

You also need to acknowledge that this environment is intended to support the library's goals and objectives, which always come first. Work, after all, is called work for a reason. The items in the preceding list are good things to have if they do not adversely affect the delivery of services.

You might ask, "How do we do this?" The first step is to *train supervisors, train supervisors, and train supervisors!* While many supervisors are very effective and well trained, others are not. Those supervisors are not malicious or evil; they just do not know how to create the culture described. They haven't been trained and they often have bad habits: habits learned from their own supervisors in their first job after graduating from library school. In many cases our profession has taken its best librarians and made them poor branch and department managers. Developing well-trained supervisors and managers is clearly the bedrock of creating a culture that supports retention. Developing a well-designed supervisory and management training program is essential, a strategy that must be adopted to ensure that the right employees are doing the right work in support of the library's goals and objectives.

Creating a Culture That Values Work/Life Balance

There are many ways to create an environment that tries to balance work with life, including the following ones. As you consider these, be mindful of what is written in your union contracts, civil service rules, and city or county policies. Not all of these strategies are possible in every library.

Define the work in terms of what is to be accomplished. Don't just say, "Our working hours are from 8 a.m. to 5 p.m. . . . be there." Unless an employee needs to cover a desk or attend meetings, focus on the project or the program. Ask: "What needs to be done?" or "What is the work?" Think about whether the work really needs to be completed on-site and only during regular business hours.

Provide flexible work schedules. Allow for job sharing and out-of-the box ways of meeting customer, employee, and library needs. Many public libraries have developed a part-time workforce to cover evening and weekend shifts. It may be that other forms of flexibility can also be accommodated. A study conducted by Catalyst showed that two-thirds—67 percent—of Generation X employees would like to work a compressed workweek, though only 6 percent actually did, and 36 percent would like to work part-time, while only 4 percent did.[8]

Provide flexible benefits plans. If possible, align what employees want with what they get. If your library controls the health benefits you offer employees, consider alternatives. Health benefits mean different things to different employees. For some, access to a fitness center is an important health benefit. For others, subsidized health screening or family insurance coverage is prized. To a still greater degree, helping employees to strike a work/life balance means tailoring paid time off and benefits to their preferences, capabilities, and level of responsibility both at home and in the library. Consider creating a cafeteria benefits plan. Look into the new consumer-driven health plans, which give employees a fixed dollar amount and make them responsible for managing their health care. While new, these plans are starting to gain acceptance.

Are your employees permitted to use sick leave to care for a sick child or parent? It's better for everyone involved if a sick leave policy recognizes this eventuality and allows employees to care for family members rather than lie about how they are using their sick leave. Have you thought of a paid time-off plan, where all time off except holiday leave is combined and employees spend it as appropriate for their needs and lifestyle? It's likely that the newer members of your workforce don't have enough vacation time, and those with many years of service can't find the time to take the time off that they earn! Paid time off can be a way to balance this equation. Figure 28 provides an illustration of one model for providing paid time off.

FIGURE 28
Paid Time Off

Paid time off (PTO) provides staff members with paid time away from work that can be used for vacation, personal time, personal illness, or time off to care for dependents. PTO takes the place of sick time, personal time, and vacation. The benefit of PTO is that it promotes a flexible approach to time off. Staff members are accountable and responsible for managing their own PTO hours to allow for adequate reserves if there is a need to cover vacation, illness or disability, appointments, emergencies, or other needs that require time off from work.

PTO must be scheduled in advance and have supervisory approval, except in the case of illness or emergency. All time away from work should be deducted from the staff member's PTO bank in hourly increments (some exceptions for exempt staff) with the exception of fixed holidays and time off in accordance with the library's policy for jury duty, military duty, or bereavement.

Accrual Example:

Years of Service	PTO Accrual
0–6 years	23 days/year or 15.33 hours/month
7 years +	28 days/year or 18.66 hours/month

The amount of accrual can be increased for senior-level positions. A specified amount of accrued hours can be carried forward at the end of the year (example: 40 hours maximum may be carried forward). When a staff member resigns, the accrued PTO can be paid to the employee.

Part-time staff members will have pro-rated PTO. For example: If a staff member works 20 hours per week, she will earn 50 percent of the above accruals.

Evaluate alternative workplaces and telecommuting as options. Most library service takes place in the library building, but there's a strong tradition of taking services outside the building as well. Think beyond bookmobiles and traditional forms of outreach services and ask yourself if all the work of the library needs to be accomplished at the library. Could telephone reference questions be answered at a more convenient location? Where do web projects need to be developed? Could question-answering and research be conducted from an employee's home? Could committee work be done by telephone or videoconference? Could e-mail and intranets be used effectively to avoid having to call a meeting at all? New technology and new definitions of acceptable work locations and activities have broadened the possibilities for answering these questions for libraries of all sizes and means.

Appreciate the dilemmas of child care, elder care, and employees playing multiple roles. The reality is that you and your employees often have family obligations. There will always be sick children, pregnancy leave, and aging and ailing parents. Accept it and to the fullest extent you can, plan for it. Recruit, train, and work to retain a qualified substitute pool (perhaps retired librarians or library school students) and treat them like valued members of your staff. Create internships or work-study programs with your local college. Create two "staff pools" of librarian and circulation staff in each region of your service area. Let employees float between branches to fill in when the need arises. Do the same for departments in your central library. Create policies and practices that anticipate and support these life-cycle events. Employees will appreciate not having to feel guilty when they must take time off to care for a child or parent.

"Allow" voluntary demotions. Your library may "allow" voluntary demotions, but it is important to create a culture where a demotion or a change of direction is safe and acceptable. What you want is a culture where an employee can take a risk and change her mind without penalty or humiliation. When Mary Sue realizes that she really doesn't like supervising employees or all the paperwork associated with an administrative position, make it easy for her to return to a job where she was competent and celebrate the fact that she tried and learned. If her former job has been filled maybe she can't return to it, but perhaps there is another vacancy that fits her and the library's needs better. She may realize that she isn't ready for a supervisory position but would like to try again in the future, or she may realize that supervision really isn't for her. Whatever she learns, it should be accepted and appreciated for what it is without a negative value being attached to it.

Appreciate the diversity of personal values and priorities. Demonstrating an acceptance of personal diversity can take a variety of forms. Accepting and supporting family obligations are one form, but there are others. Increasingly, HR specialists are writing about the employees without family responsibilities who want time to do what interests them. Their interests might range from taking windsurfing lessons to traveling, performing a community service, or taking a class. Could this time be built into the employee's and library's schedule? If not, why not? Paid time off and personal leave options might encourage both the recruitment and retention of the high-performers who want a position that allows them to pursue personal interests.

Wonderful ideas, you say. But how can I implement them in my library? My library operates under the mandates of our local jurisdiction. "No creativity allowed here!" is the refrain heard in between the lines when we suggest a new program. Don't despair. There are ways to have your voice heard, but it will take some time and work. Here are some tips.

1. Get involved. If your local jurisdiction is creating a bargaining team, studying benefits, or assessing the workforce or the climate of employees, volunteer to serve on the committee. You will learn what is happening, and a great deal more; you will be the "go to" person for issues pertaining to the library's workforce; and most important, you will gain their respect, so that they will listen to your suggestions when you want to try something new.

2. Take the long view. Most local jurisdictions are bureaucratic, and changing the course, even allowing for some flexibility, can take a considerable amount of time.

3. In the meantime, keep reinforcing your credibility and stay in dialogue. Be a team player and don't bad-mouth the process or the bureaucracy. Remember, when you are ready, you want them to accept your ideas at least provisionally, if not enthusiastically.

4. When you see the time is right, meet with the HR director of your local jurisdiction. Turn her into an ally. Be prepared. Share the information you learned from this book, other resources, and conferences. Anticipate resistance. Have answers to the questions she will ask that pertain to best practices for recruitment and retention as well as to how your plan for workforce flexibility fits in to the library and its workforce. Offer to sponsor it as a pilot, so the local jurisdiction doesn't have to make a complete policy change. Tell the HR director that you will share the library's learning and even help make a case to the county executive, civil service commission, union, staff association, or other group.

Being part of the team and understanding your local jurisdiction's needs and resources will make you a valuable member of that team. You will learn and understand its needs as well. You will then be able to clearly articulate your case in a way that would make it difficult for anyone to turn you down!

Step 5.4
Define Expectations

It seems obvious, but performance problems are frequently the result of the work not being clearly defined. It is very critical for the employee to have clear answers to the following questions:

> What is my job?
>
> What must I accomplish?
>
> To what level of quality/quantity/time frame?
>
> How will I know I've been successful?
>
> What resources are available to help me (including the supervisor, the library's intranet, city/county/library resources online, a mentor, the HR department, training materials, peers, etc.)?

Most employees just want to be told "the bookends," that is, the scope of the work. What needs to be done? What are the expected results or outcomes? Tell them, and then let them put their own imprint on "how" the work gets done.

Many supervisors have a hard time letting go of the "how" to do the job. These supervisors have done the job for a long time and just "know" the best way. While it may be the best way for the supervisor, the new employee might have a better way, or at least a way that works really well for her . . . and fulfills her individual performance plan (Workform 8). An individual performance plan lists the activities each employee will engage in over the course of the year in order to fulfill assigned goals linking to the library's service priorities. It lists the time frame for accomplishing each activity, the measures of success for it, and any resources that will be needed.

Rewards and Incentives

Motivated workers make the difference between failure and success, turnover and loyalty. What employees want most is interesting work and appreciation for their efforts. Lack of recognition or appreciation is one of the top reasons why high-performing employees leave their jobs. Yet many employers neglect to use this simple management tool.

Some libraries create written, formal recognition programs. For the most part, simplicity reigns. A library leader saying a sincere, personal "Thank you!" to the employee is great, especially if done on the spot or at the time of the accomplishment. Referencing a specific accomplishment adds value. Sending a handwritten thank-you note to an employee is silver medal territory, and offering a specific "Thank you" in front of other employees is gold. Celebrate a library accomplishment as a group and you've hit platinum.

Over the years, recognition programs have changed. Until recently they were formal, centrally (HR) run, infrequent, based in cultures of entitlement, and selectively used for the few very top performers. The norm now is multiple recognition programs and activities that are leader-oriented, informal, frequent, and flexible. They are shaped by cultures of performance and are available to reward everyone.

If your library does not have a recognition program, you'll be amazed to see how productivity and morale increase by implementing even the simplest one. A few guidelines for starting a program are

Make the program meaningful; the things that are recognized should be worthwhile and not trivial.

Focus on the areas that have the most impact.

Involve employees.

Develop clear, objective criteria and recognize all who hit them.

Develop the logistics (i.e., schedules, time frames of events).

Announce the program with fanfare.

Publicly track progress; "if you don't measure it, you can't manage it!"

Have lots of winners.

Allow flexibility of rewards.

Renew the program as needed; build on successes and learn from mistakes.

Link informal and formal rewards.

The program can be low-cost and still yield high-impact results. A medium-sized public library offers "Everyone Counts" spot awards which can be used for video coupons, branch sale items (such as tote bags), store gift cards, book sale items, summer reading T-shirts, or books sold at the circulation desk. The vouchers are valued at $1.50 each and can be accumulated for a larger item. A supervisor or coworker can hand one to any employee on the spot. Ten-dollar vouchers for a gift basket, breakfast, or gift card are also presented on the spot to employees who handle an emergency or a difficult librarian-in-charge situation, fill in on another job, complete a special task, or consistently present a positive attitude that inspires or gives time and assistance to an area or staff person outside the assigned department or area of responsibility. This library system also provides more formal incentives and recognition with its Customer Service Spirit and Service awards twice a year. The awards are $200, and two each are presented at Staff Day each year.

In addition to providing formal awards, a large public library offers "Applause" awards that are spontaneous and can be given at any time by any employee to any other employee. They are awarded as a way to say "Thank you!" for going beyond expectations and doing a great job. These are used to say, "I know the terrific job you did/are doing and I appreciate your efforts." These spot awards consist of a certificate and a $5 gift or premium. This system also offers two large incentive awards ($500) for employees who demonstrate an ongoing commitment to quality customer service, create a major project, practice innovative thinking resulting in a significant improvement in library operations or customer services, are willing to undertake new responsibilities or to participate in activities not usually included in the job description, or produce an extremely high volume of quality work output over an extended period of time.

Other libraries provide suggestion programs with cost savings shared by the employee and library. You can also have celebratory bragging sessions where employees share their progress with library leadership; start staff meetings with good news and praise for employees who deserve it; read thank-you letters from customers; schedule self-recognition or recognition days; or send a card on an employee's anniversary date noting her accomplishments for the year and how important the person is to the department. You are limited only by your creativity. If you need a boost, read *1001 Ways to Reward Employees.*[9] It will help spur your creativity. Recognition programs are a very low-cost way to show employees respect and appreciation. They focus on performance, help make work fun, and lead to retention of top talent.

Step 5.5
Provide Training

When you hear the words *staff development* you probably think of formal training programs, and these are certainly an important component of staff development. However, they are not the only component. Developing your employees starts with orientation and doesn't end until retirement. It includes both formal and informal learning opportunities and it focuses on the needs of individual employees.

An employee's experience and impression of a place start with recruitment; that is, before he or she is actually hired. The information in chapter 4 will help create a good first impression. Recruitment, orientation, and assimilation processes provide chances to emphasize the personal elements of a prospective employee's connection to the organization.

Employee Orientation

Orienting new employees to the library and their job continues to be one of the most ignored functions in libraries. Too often it is not conducted at all, and when it is, it is often done poorly: paperwork overload, boring lectures, and overwhelming amounts of information. Too often the new employee is left to sink or swim. New employee orientation should be conducted within the first thirty days of employment.

WHY CONDUCT AN ORIENTATION PROGRAM?

Orientation is not just a "nice to have" function. Since new employees make their decision to stay or leave the library within their first ninety days, it is an important component of the recruitment and retention effort and serves several key purposes:

1. To make the employee feel welcome and help her get up to speed on the job quickly
2. To reduce the employee's anxiety about the new job and eliminate the stress of guessing how she should respond to easy-to-answer questions
3. To reduce turnover by showing that the library values the employee and provides the tools for success
4. To save the time of managers and peers by providing consistent information that all employees need
5. To develop realistic job expectations, convey an understanding of the library's values and goals, and help the employee see where she fits into this picture

There are two types of orientations, and both should be provided: an overview of the library and an overview of the job.[10] The first provides the basic information a new employee needs to get started and includes detail on the library and its context in local government, the employee's department or branch, important policies, information about compensation and benefits, safety issues, employee and union issues, and physical facilities. This type of orientation can be conducted by the human resources department or by a skilled librarian or other staff person, since it is generic information that is not related to any one job.

The second type of orientation must be handled by the supervisor or manager. It pertains to the library's goals and how the employee and her job fits in: her job responsibilities, performance expectations, and duties; policies and procedures; how the supervisor likes to work with and communicate with employees; and an introduction to coworkers and others. Workform 11, New Employee Orientation, provides a detailed outline of an orientation program that addresses both types of orientations and the assimilation of the new employee into the library.

You should consider completing paperwork and procedural tasks before the new employee orientation. That allows the employee to actually think about what she is experiencing during the orientation rather than worrying about all of the paperwork details that accompany a new job. If the employee is moving to your area, helping with relocation, inviting the new hire to introduce her family to the library and vice versa, and matching her with local services (e.g., babysitters) foster the sort of personal connections that most employees value.

The orientation should include basic elements (introducing the new employee to co-workers, having the work space ready, providing instruction on the use of office equipment and basic information about where to put coats, lunches, etc.) as well as the employee's specific job and a more general orientation to the library as a whole. Creating a checklist of points to cover can be helpful to the harried manager, so that both the most mundane and the most critical points can be remembered. Adding a few extra touches (balloons at the desk, a mug with the library's logo, the director stopping by to introduce herself) can make the new employee feel even more welcome and valued. One director sends a "welcome card" to new employees. She writes in it: "At the end of some days you'll feel elated; after some you'll feel completely drained; but may you always leave the library knowing you contributed to our organization!"

It can be helpful to survey new employees to get their reactions to the orientation after they have been on the job for 30, 60, or 120 days. Share the feedback with library leadership and then make adjustments to the orientation process as needed. That way you can improve your library's induction process while also communicating to new hires that their input is valued. First impressions are extremely important, and taking the time to find out if the library is making a positive and productive first impression will pay off in increased feelings of inclusion and loyalty.

Going beyond surveying reactions to orientation is an important next step. Talk to employees about what they are doing and about their thoughts and feelings toward the library and their job. Managers and peers could also provide important information about what is going well and what is not. Rather than leaving it to chance, assign a staff member to this function. Taking the time to interact in a genuine way with new employees is vital. Research shows that most new employees decide within their first ninety days if they will remain on the job.

A new employee's assimilation into the library workplace can be enhanced through consciously acknowledging this process and developing standards and practices that support it. Managers need to know that they are expected to assist new employees throughout their first few months of employment by purposefully creating ways for them to become engaged members of their branch or work unit. Publicizing and recognizing creative ways of doing this can inspire other supervisors and managers and create an environment that is seen to value the thoughtful induction of new employees.

TIPS FOR DESIGNING AN ORIENTATION PROGRAM

Workform 11 will help you plan an orientation program that develops loyalty, enhances morale, and supports retention. It also reinforces the fact that you must consciously plan a new employee's introduction to your library and make sure that someone is assigned to each piece of the orientation process. This workform (or any other orientation form) should be reviewed and updated regularly in order to ensure its continued accuracy and relevance.

However, before redesigning or creating an orientation program, gather input from employees (both long-term and those recently hired), managers, and others and ask the following questions:

> What does the new employee need to know about this library and its work environment to make her feel more comfortable?

What impression do we want to make on the employee's first day?

What key policies and procedures must the employee be aware of to avoid mistakes in her first weeks and months of hire? Focus on key issues.

What special things (desk, work area, equipment, special instructions) should be provided to make the new employee feel comfortable, welcome, and secure?

What specific things can supervisors and managers do so the employee begins to know her coworkers?

What positive experience can I provide for new employees that they could discuss with their families? The experience should be something to make the new employee feel valued by the library.[11]

What can we do to make sure this process is fun and welcoming?

Strategies for Developing Staff

Whether your library is large or small, there are a number of things you might consider to help your staff grow and develop. Keep in mind any programs provided by your jurisdiction, as well as requirements in your civil service rules or union contract. These programs include the following.

Grow your own workforce. Provide support for employees seeking a bachelor's degree or an MLS. Give tuition assistance to employees who are working full-time while attending college or library school (any little bit helps), as well as some time off to study every week. Just an hour or two makes a huge difference to a working student.

Promote MLS students to an interim job-grade level. After the student has successfully completed half of her degree program, reclassify her job from library associate to librarian trainee or another title. Award a grade increase, as well as a salary increase. The employee will value your appreciation and show it in her work, as well as in her loyalty and her decision to remain in the library after graduation.

Develop a program of job rotation and cross-training. Have staff swap jobs for three to six months. All will return with increased job knowledge, vitality, perspective, and appreciation of the library, its work, and workforce. Do it as part of a structured program where the staff keep a journal or record questions they encounter and discuss the key things they have learned with their peers or a coach.

Job rotation does not have to be this extensive. Alternatively, you can rotate library associates assigned to the central library into a branch for a week or rotate employees among branches, if you have more than one building. Cross-train public service, technical services, and business office employees. Not only will these assignments develop the individuals involved, but cross-training provides the library with a more flexible and capable workforce, eliminating work stoppages or backlogs when a vacation is taken or someone is out on extended sick leave.

Develop employees by asking them to serve on task forces or in interim job assignments. Do not repeatedly ask the same people to serve on task forces or committees. For each new task force or job assignment, seek out a promising person who hasn't been given an opportunity to participate. Ask her to serve. If she agrees, provide support and watch her blossom.

Implement a 360-degree feedback program. In a 360-degree feedback program, performance data is obtained from peers, subordinates, and the supervisor in order to provide an assessment of an employee's performance up, down, and sideways in the organization. It provides full circle, or 360-degree, feedback. This type of evaluation process offers employees a learning tool and feedback mechanism to promote employee growth and development. There are a variety of ways to conduct a 360-degree feedback program. As with other approaches to employee performance evaluation, it is essential that everyone involved understand the purposes of the evaluation and receive thorough training in applying the process.

Create a dual career-ladder system for librarians. Career ladders allow employees to focus on their expertise as an individual contributor (e.g., a children's librarian) without having to take on a management role to earn more money. In this scenario, an employee might advance from Librarian I to II by taking on more responsibility in collection development, conducting research, or designing new programs in early childhood learning. Other options might include the Librarian I moving up by becoming a specialist in literacy readers' advisory, information technology, or training. There are many ways to acknowledge and reward your staff for increasing their responsibility and value to the library outside of advancement to a management position.

While the library might ultimately place the employee in a higher grade level and pay her a higher salary, that amount will be far less than the cost of replacing her if she goes elsewhere, or the cost of low morale and mistakes if she takes a management job she doesn't really desire just to earn more money.

Assign mentors to both new and longer-term employees. This is especially important when an employee is promoted or assumes a new role. Mentoring can be a powerful tool in employee development. An effective mentoring process takes some thought and preplanning. It is important to match the mentor and the mentee carefully. Their personal styles and interests should be compatible. Allow a trial period for the relationship to settle in, and if there are problems, make needed adjustments.

You will want to identify clear expectations for the mentoring relationship. Define the results you expect and discuss responsibilities, roles, and expectations with both the mentor and mentee. Provide training for mentors. Monitor and evaluate progress and reset expectations as the relationship grows and changes. The formal mentor/mentee relationship is not intended to be permanent. The last phase of the formal relationship should be to encourage independence at the appropriate time. Lois Zachary's *The Mentor's Guide: Facilitating Effective Learning Relationships* is a wonderful resource for developing a mentoring program or relationship.[12]

Step 5.6
Build Commitment

The suggestions in Step 5.5 will help you build a workforce of competent and effective staff members. Every organization wants to retain the best and brightest members of its staff, but that is becoming increasingly difficult. Today's employees are more mobile than ever before. The typical employee starting in the workforce now will have seven or more jobs in her lifetime and in several different careers. Library managers need to think about ways to build commitment in their employees.

Exit Interviews

Employees may leave for other, possibly higher-level or more lucrative library jobs, for jobs in other sectors, or for retirement or personal reasons. Managers should learn from each situation. Exit interviews can provide an invaluable source of information, especially when an employee is leaving for a job in another library system. Managers need to learn more about what prompted a resignation. What pull did another job have, or what pushed the employee to leave her current job? If you are having trouble retaining key staff, carefully and systematically explore the causes. Losing staff is a symptom. Doing something about it demands an understanding of the true causes.

The exit interview should be performed by human resources staff, an ombudsperson, or a neutral person. The employee should be assured that the information she shares will be confidential and used only as summary feedback to help improve retention at the library. The exit interview should not be conducted by the employee's supervisor or anyone in her chain of command, in case supervision or leadership is the reason the person is leaving the library's employment. Even in large libraries, to the extent possible, you should conduct exit interviews of employees at all levels, including pages and clerks. All those separating from the library at their choice can be an important source of information about library and management practices, as well as compensation, benefits, and the work environment. While face-to-face interviews may elicit more information, they are more time-consuming and harder to schedule. An online survey, hosted on the library's intranet or by SurveyMonkey.com or some other source, is a realistic alternative and may even provide more candid information.

Workform 12, Exit Interview Questionnaire, will guide you through the exit interview process.

Employee Climate Surveys

Not waiting until employees leave to solicit their opinions about life and work at the library is a proactive way to understand the wants and needs of your workforce. Many organizations (and a few public libraries) conduct confidential employee climate or opinion surveys and make changes based upon what they discover. You can study a variety of issues, depending on the conditions in your library. The typical topics involved in how employees think and feel about their workplace include

- job satisfaction
- leadership
- training
- compensation and benefits
- technology and tools
- customer services
- communications and information received
- supervision
- understanding the library's vision and service priorities
- job expectations

Conducting a climate study is not as daunting as you might think. Start by creating and chartering a "climate study" committee. Include a cross-section of employees and managers on the committee. Invite representatives from branches, the central library, technical services, business services, and the union or staff association, as well as newer employees, long-term employees, women, men, people of color, and so on. Strive for diversity on this committee. Clarify if it is an advisory or a steering committee in terms of the types of decisions the group will be authorized to make. Chapter 1 of this book has more information on appointing committees, and Workform 1 will help you develop a committee charter.

Decide what topics you wish to study and how you plan to collect the data. Will some members of the committee conduct interviews or focus groups? Will you use a consultant or local faculty member to help? What about collecting quantitative data via a web-based survey? You could easily pick a handful of topics and ask 10 to 20 questions on your intranet. If confidentiality is a concern, go to SurveyMonkey.com. For a very low fee, you can purchase one or two months of this resource. SurveyMonkey, Zoomerang, and other web-based survey companies will walk you through the design of the survey and will also tabulate the data.

Write the questions to include in your survey. Think carefully about what you want to know. It is easy to tabulate and analyze data from multiple-choice questions, but it is much more challenging to code, tabulate, and analyze data from open-ended questions. Now is the time to decide how you want to understand the survey responses when it comes time to analyze the data. Do you want to be able to look at answers by department, branch, or unit, by gender, race, tenure, age? If so, you have to ask the respondents to identify themselves by those categories when they are taking the survey.

Always test the questions in your survey with a small group of the people who will be taking the survey before you distribute the survey to the entire staff. You may be surprised by how differently respondents interpret questions that you thought were perfectly clear. After the pilot test, review the surveys and talk to the people who were your testers. Ask them if they understood the survey instructions and if the questions were clear. You might also ask if the testers want to tell you about something that was not included in the survey. Revise the survey and ask the testers to review the revised questions to make sure they reflect the needed changes.

When the survey instrument is finalized, you are ready to publicize and conduct the survey. Communication should be sent from the library director letting employees know who the members of the committee are, the purpose of the survey, and what will be done with the data. Confidentiality should be stressed, as should the commitment by the director to review and implement findings as feasible. Implementation issues and approaches will depend on the purpose of the survey.

After the closing date for returns, you are ready to analyze the data and act on what you learn. Always report the survey results to employees, even if the results are not positive. If you don't report the results of a survey, you can be sure that the grapevine will assume the worst and employees will resent your starting a project without bringing it to closure. Use simple bar graphs and pie charts to show the data to employees. Start by asking them if there are any surprises or anything missing in the results. Get employees involved in making changes suggested by the survey data.

The director should also provide one-to-one feedback on departmental findings to each department head. Based upon their feedback, the committee and director should plan and prioritize next steps and develop an action plan. Keep the committee active as action is taken and changes are made, or if appropriate, appoint new committees to manage projects that result from the survey. Review lessons learned at every stage; celebrate, monitor, evaluate, and survey employees again. Making changes based on what you learn from the survey can be a powerful force for showing employees that you value what they say. As a result, it creates a culture that is conducive to retention. Whenever possible, it is often best to hire outside consultants to do these kinds of surveys. The outsiders have more credibility and the staff is often more comfortable about confidentiality issues.

There are four tool kits in *Demonstrating Results: Using Outcome Measurement in Your Library* that will also be helpful as you develop, tabulate, and analyze your surveys: Tool Kit C, Sample Confidentiality Forms; Tool Kit D, Tips on Developing Questionnaires; Tool Kit E, Data Preparation, Coding, and Processing; and Tool Kit F, Sampling.[13]

Retaining Talent as They Age

Phased retirement is an important way to mitigate the impact of employee exit on the library. By making schedules and tasks more flexible for those considering retirement, managers can retain a talented pool of mentors. In a phased-in retirement or as retirees, former full-time employees can provide a reliable, flexible, knowledgeable, and affordable addition to the library's workforce.

Inducements could include flexible hours or assignments so that retirees can travel or pursue other personal interests but still be available during parts of the year, parts of the week, or for projects of several months' duration. Some library employers are finding ways to capture and celebrate the many years of experience and the deep knowledge base their most senior employees possess. Others are developing ways for senior staff and managers to take longer periods of time off while still retaining their employment status, or to phase out by working part-time or on temporary assignments before they ultimately retire completely. This latter option is most attractive when future retirement benefits are not adversely impacted by such preretirement reductions in hours.

Retirees can be a great source of desk coverage or coaching. Keep them informed and connected. Have them work in an on-call arrangement. Give them a cell phone, a computer, and a coaching assignment!

You should review your local government's civil service rules and personnel policies to ensure that retirees can continue to work. Retirement rules vary by state and local jurisdiction. In some locales, retirees cannot continue to work at all in the organization from which they retired. It is considered to be "double dipping" from the local government. In other jurisdictions it is acceptable, and in other instances where full-time work is not permitted, hourly or consulting work is allowed, so check the details, as well as the regulations pertaining to benefits, pensions, maximum salary permissible, and so on. Provide assistance to these employees through local financial planners or retirement counselors to ensure that they are comfortable with the arrangements, particularly if they are able to collect Social Security.

The Keys to Commitment

A responsive work environment is a crucial source of employee commitment and thus retention. The keywords here are

- communication
- accountability
- recognition

Creating and maintaining effective forums for employee input can connect leaders to staff at all levels. Employee involvement in decision-making, made possible by open but structured communication, invests everyone in positive and negative outcomes, such that all are accountable to all. Finally, accountability is inseparable from recognition for contributions and achievements. Whether it is just a "Thank you" and applause at a staff meeting or a promotion or some other substantial acknowledgment, the universality of forms of recognition in public- and private-sector organizations is a testament to recognition's importance for cementing employee commitment.

These strategies are all about building commitment to the job and the employer, since productivity and retention are greatly increased when employees are committed. Retention strategies must be intentionally designed so that employees know what they need to do and what is expected of them; are involved in decisions that impact the work they do and the services they provide; have opportunities to learn and grow; receive recognition for good performance; and know they are responsible for their performance and are held accountable if performance is lacking. Strategies developed with these factors in mind will result in the best and brightest employees choosing to stay with the library that allows them to contribute, learn, and grow.

In sum, productivity and employee retention are greatly increased when employees are committed. This is especially important today, since job security and loyalty to an employer are lower than ever. To enhance retention, remember these five keys:

1. *Focus.* Employees know what they need to do and what is expected of them.
2. *Involvement.* People support most what they help to create.
3. *Development.* Opportunities for learning and growth are encouraged.
4. *Gratitude.* Recognition (formal or informal) is given for good performance.
5. *Accountability.* Employees are responsible for their performance.

Conclusion

This book, written for public libraries as part of the Results series, is designed to help library administrators and human resources staff become strategic in their efforts to improve library performance, fulfill the library's strategic goals and service priorities, and effectively recruit, retain, and motivate a high-performing workforce. Making changes based on the processes described in this book should help your library achieve maximum productivity, sustain a competitive advantage, provide a balanced quality of work and life for employees, capitalize on workforce adaptability to meet the needs of both the employees and the library . . . and in short . . . achieve results!

To this end, we discussed the HR trends that will be affecting your library very soon, if they haven't already. We showed you the difference between tactical (day-to-day transactional) and strategic HR practices that lead to results in the library. We suggested a number of projects you should begin that will allow strategic human resources to become a transformational force in achieving library results.

Some of the practices we suggested include the following: identify and support excellent people-management practices; provide metrics to library managers, thus putting them in a stronger position to respond to trends and to forecast future situations that will affect the library's ability to carry out its service goals; develop effective communications; recruit proactively; retain top performers; provide employee challenges; and engage in strategic planning. We hope you find these and other practices and projects suggested in this book to be important and valuable in supporting your library's quest for results.

Notes

1. Marcus Cunningham and Curt Coffman, *First Break All the Rules: What the World's Greatest Managers Do Differently* (New York: Simon and Schuster, 1999).

2. Christi Olson and Paula Singer, *Winning with Library Leadership: Enhancing Services through Connection, Contribution, and Collaboration* (Chicago: American Library Association, 2004).

3. Ibid.

4. Lynne C. Lancaster and David Stillman, *When Generations Collide: Who They Are, Why They Clash, How to Solve the Generational Puzzle at Work* (New York: HarperCollins, 2002).

5. D. Doverspike and A. O'Malley, "When Generations Collide: Part 1," International Public Management Association for Human Resources newsletter, February 2006. http://www.ipma-hr.org.

6. Doug Brown, "Understanding Four Generations in the Workplace," *Fort Worth Business Press,* June 27, 2003, 11.

7. Carolyn A. Martin, "Bridging the Generation Gap(s)," *Nursing* 34, no. 12 (December 2004): 62–63.

8. Catalyst, Inc., "Workplace Flexibility Isn't Just a Women's Issue," *Viewpoints,* August 2003. http://www.catalyst.org/files/view/Workplace%20Flexibility%20Isn%27t%20Just%20a%20Women%27s%20Issue.pdf.

9. Bob Nelson, *1001 Ways to Reward Employees,* 2nd ed. (New York: Workman, 2005).

10. Bacal and Associates, "A Quick Guide to Employee Orientation—Help for Managers and HR," http://www.work911.com/articles/orient.htm.

11. Judith Brown "Employee Orientation: Keeping New Employees on Board," http://humanresources.about.com/od/retention/a/keepnewemployee.htm.

12. Lois Zachary, *The Mentor's Guide: Facilitating Effective Learning Relationships* (San Francisco: Jossey-Bass, 2000).

13. Rhea Joyce Rubin, *Demonstrating Results: Using Outcome Measurement in Your Library* (Chicago: American Library Association, 2006), 104–12.

Workforms

Instructions

Purpose of Workform 1

Use this workform to define the purpose of the project committee. A project committee may be created to manage, review, or provide advice on a variety of projects described in this book.

Sources of Data for Workform 1

The project purpose, resources, budget, etc., are the sources of the data for this workform.

Factors to Consider When Completing Workform 1

1. The intent of the project should be unambiguous and provide a clear statement of what you expect to accomplish. For example, a library planning on devising an employee performance management plan might write this purpose statement:

   "Create a performance management process that links to the library's strategic plan and clearly defines activities and expectations for employees."

2. Carefully consider the resources that will be necessary to successfully complete the project. The charge provides a clear outline of expectations, scope, resources, time line, and possible limitations.

To Complete Workform 1

1. **Row A.** Indicate the committee's name.

2. **Row B.** Identify the purpose of the project committee.

3. **Row C.** Provide the time line for the project. Include starting date, ending date, and dates of any milestones in the project.

4. **Row D.** List the project results or deliverables. These will also provide a picture of what the committee will accomplish and the project's scope.

5. **Row E.**

   E1: Provide an itemized budget for the project (for consultants, etc.).

   E2: Who will facilitate committee meetings?

   E3: Describe the meeting space and equipment the committee will need to do its work.

   E4: Describe the administrative and computer support that will be provided, if any.

   E5: Estimate the time commitment for the project committee members.

   E6: List any expert resources from inside or outside the organization that should be included.

   E7: List any other resource issues that are unique to your project.

6. **Row F.** Describe the project committee's accountability and authority parameters (that is, whether the committee is advisory, its reporting structure, etc.). There might be confidentiality considerations or there might be approval steps that committee members and others need to be aware of.

7. Complete the information at the bottom of the form:

   Completed by Enter the name of the person or persons who completed the workform.

   Source of data Indicate the source of the data used to complete the workform.

   Date completed Enter the date the workform was completed.

   Library Enter the library's name.

Factors to Consider When Reviewing Workform 1

1. Have you reviewed the purpose of the project to be sure that you understand what it is?

2. Is the time line realistic?

3. Are the deliverables clearly described?

4. Have you identified the resources that will be available to the committee members and the time line for the completion of the project?

5. Have you provided enough information to ensure that the project committee's members clearly understand their authority and the reporting structure in which they will operate?

A. Committee Name: _____

B. Purpose of Committee:

C. Committee Time Line:

D. Project Deliverables: Specifically, what is the committee expected to produce?

1.

2.

3.

4.

E. Resources:

1. Budget:

2. Facilitation:

3. Meeting and working space and equipment:

4. Administrative and computer support:

5. Time commitment required of committee members:

6. Expert resources:

7. Other:

F. Accountability and Authority:

Completed by _____ Date completed _____

Source of data _____ Library _____

Instructions

Purpose of Workform 2

Use this workform to determine what staff resources will be required to accomplish specific activities. These staff resources will be full-time, part-time or hourly employees or, possibly, contract employees or consultants hired to do necessary work to achieve the library's strategic goals and objectives.

Sources of Data for Workform 2

Information about current staffing allocations (number of full-time equivalents ([FTEs] or hours allocated per week) will be available as part of the library's personnel and budget system. You may have to estimate the number of hours needed to carry out a specific activity (such as planning and conducting a special event). In addition to the hours available, you'll also need to assess the knowledge, skills, abilities, and competencies available to implement the activities you wish to carry out. For example, you might determine that you need someone who is bilingual and bicultural to provide outreach services to the Spanish-speaking members of your community. You would want the ability to speak Spanish as well as the ability to interact comfortably with the local Spanish-speaking community.

Factors to Consider When Completing Workform 2

1. Carefully consider the knowledge, skills, abilities, and competencies needed. Think beyond traditional job descriptions and formal education and experience to consider what you need done and what the person being considered for the activity has accomplished in past jobs and other experiences, such as volunteer work, internships, etc.

To Complete Workform 2

1. **Section A.** Indicate the activity that staffing is being analyzed for.
2. **Section B.** Define the staff resource required to carry out that activity. If there is more than one, fill out a workform for each staff resource.
3. **Section C.** Describe what you think you need in terms of knowledge, skills, abilities, and competencies and FTEs or hours.

4. **Section D.** Describe your current staff resources in terms of hours available or FTE and knowledge, skills, abilities, and competencies.
5. **Section E.** Define the gap between what you have and what you need. For example, you might have a .5 FTE (that is, half-time) children's librarian but without any Spanish language skills or experience working with community groups other than the local schools. You may feel you need a full-time person who has language and cultural proficiencies and is also experienced in doing community development work. If you find you have more of a staffing resource than is needed, define the surplus.
6. **Section F.** Describe the plan for filling the gap or reallocating the surplus.
7. Complete the information at the bottom of the form:

   Completed by Enter the name of the person or persons who completed the workform.

   Source of data Indicate the source of the data used to complete the workform.

   Date completed Enter the date the workform was completed.

   Library Enter the library's name.

Factors to Consider When Reviewing Workform 2

1. Have you reviewed the goals and objectives of your strategic plan to be sure that the activity under consideration is a good choice as an implementation activity?
2. Have you identified the human resources that will be necessary to successfully implement the activity? Have you considered the amount of time you need and the knowledge, skills, abilities, and competencies necessary to carry out the selected activity?
3. Is your plan for filling the gap or reallocating a surplus for this particular activity realistic? Have you identified ways to eliminate or streamline tasks to free up time that can be devoted to this activity?

A. Activity

B. Staff resource required to accomplish activity

C. Need	**D. Have**	**E. Gap/Surplus**
Knowledge	Knowledge	Knowledge
Skills	Skills	Skills
Abilities	Abilities	Abilities
Hours or FTE	Hours or FTE	Hours or FTE

F. Plan for filling the gap or reallocating the surplus

Completed by _____   Date completed _____

Source of data _____   Library _____

Instructions

Purpose of Workform 3

The purpose of this questionnaire is to gather information about an employee's job.

Sources of Data for Workform 3

Depending on the number of employees the library has, every employee may be asked to fill out the PDQ or only a representative sample. If a sample is used, be sure to include employees in different locations within the library. Supervisors and managers who review the forms should be knowledgeable about the work that their subordinates perform.

Factors to Consider When Completing Workform 3

1. Provide employees with an orientation to the PDQ so they know how to fill it out and what will be done with the information provided.

2. The PDQ job summary and job duty list should be a summary and a listing of the basic, essential duties of a job, not an exhaustive listing of everything an employee does.

3. Fill out the form in a way that reflects normal job duties currently being performed, rather than special projects or assignments or duties that are expected to be done in the future.

4. Complete every section accurately and thoroughly, without either understating or inflating answers. Do not use acronyms or abbreviations.

5. Feel free to provide examples or attach comments or additional materials to any section.

To Complete Workform 3

1. **Section A.** Fill out each line with appropriate information.

2. **Section B.** Briefly describe the purpose of the job. One or two sentences should answer the question: Why does this position exist?

3. **Section C.** List the major duties and responsibilities of the job, including the percentage of time spent on the duty.

4. **Section D.** Answer every question in this section. If no response exactly matches the job, choose the one that reflects the job 90 percent or more of the time.

5. **Section E.** The person who supervises the job fills out this section, answering each question and providing additional comments, if necessary.

Factors to Consider When Reviewing Workform 3

1. Check to be sure that all questions have been answered. Follow up with the employee if information is missing.

2. Seek clarification if employees who seem to be doing the same work answer in significantly different ways. There may be actual differences in major job duties or the percentage of time spent on job duties, or there may be differences in how employees perceive their jobs or how they express themselves when writing about their jobs.

POSITION DESCRIPTION QUESTIONNAIRE

Introduction

The purpose of this questionnaire is to gather information about your job. We are asking you to complete the questionnaire because you know the most about your job. Your answers, responses from other employees, and your supervisor's comments will serve as the basis for

- summarizing key position information;
- ensuring that all jobs are accurately assessed; and
- determining how jobs within the library compare to each other.

Instructions

- Complete the questionnaire with your job in mind, not your personal characteristics or performance.

- Before you begin to answer the questions, please take a few minutes to read through the entire questionnaire, reading all instructions carefully.

- Once you begin to answer the questions, be as objective as possible, responding about your job and not your personal situation or performance. Remember, it is your position, not your performance, that is being reviewed.

- As you respond to the questions, your answers should reflect

   what would normally be expected of someone fully trained in the job, rather than a beginner or someone performing over and above what is required;

   the expected or normal routine of the job rather than special projects, temporary assignments, or out-of-the ordinary occurrences; and

   the job as it is today, rather than what you expect it to become in the future.

- Complete each section accurately and thoroughly. Try not to understate or inflate your answers. Please do not use acronyms or abbreviations.

- Choose the best response for your job. If no response exactly matches your job, choose *the one* that reflects your job 90 percent or more of the time.

- Answer every question.

- Provide examples.

- Feel free to write comments in any section and to attach additional materials if necessary.

After you have completed this questionnaire, please give it to your supervisor by _____.
[DATE]

If you have any questions, please contact _____.
[CONTACT PERSON]

Thank you for your participation.

(Cont.)

WORKFORM 3 **Position Description Questionnaire** (Cont.)

A. Name: _____

Job title: _____

Work location: _____

Full-time: _____

How long in current position: _____

Part-time: _____

Number of hours per week: _____

B. Position Summary

Describe the purpose of your job in your own language. This should be just one or two sentences that answer the question: Why does this position exist?

(Cont.)

WORKFORM 3 **Position Description Questionnaire** (Cont.)

C. Duties and Responsibilities

List the major duties of your job and indicate the percentage of time you spend on each duty. For example, you might list "Check in returned library materials" as a major job duty and indicate that 40 percent of your time is spent on this duty.

Job Duty	Percentage of Time
TOTAL:	100%

(Cont.)

D. Describe the type and extent of supervision you receive:

_____

_____

_____

Do you supervise anyone else? If so, please list by job title. If you supervise more than one person with the same title, indicate the number in parentheses after the job title.

_____

_____

Which of the following supervisory duties do you perform if you do supervise someone else (circle those that apply):

- Training
- Performance appraisal
- Budgeting
- Coaching/counseling
- Inspecting work
- Other: _____

What education level do you think the job requires?

_____

_____

What amount of experience do you think is needed to perform the job? Answer in months or years. _____

What equipment, tools, machines, or work aids are used to perform the job?

_____

_____

Are there any personal attributes (special aptitudes, physical characteristics, personality traits, etc.) required by the job?

_____

_____

Thank you for the information you've provided.

(Cont.)

WORKFORM 3 **Position Description Questionnaire** (Cont.)

E. Supervisor's Comments

This portion of the questionnaire is to be completed by your supervisor.

As a supervisor, it is important that you review this questionnaire and identify any discrepancies between the employee's responses and your own knowledge of the job. Remember, this questionnaire is intended solely for the purpose of accurately describing the position and not the individual or his/her performance.

If you would like to add a note or suggest a correction to any answer, please do so next to the employee's answer and identify your entry with your printed initials, without changing the employee's answer. In addition, please complete the following:

1. Do you agree with the answers provided by the employee? If not, please explain.

_____

_____

_____

_____

2. List any important job duties this person performs that may have been omitted. Please add under the appropriate section as well.

_____

_____

_____

_____

_____

3. Additional comments:

_____

_____

_____

_____

_____

_____   _____
SUPERVISOR'S NAME   SUPERVISOR'S TITLE

_____   _____
SUPERVISOR'S SIGNATURE   DATE

_____   _____
DEPARTMENT DIRECTOR   DATE

Completed by _____   Date completed _____

Source of data _____   Library _____

Instructions

WORKFORM 4 **Job Description Template**

Purpose of Workform 4

Use this form as a template to create a job description.

Sources of Data for Workform 4

The information you gather from performing the job analysis will provide the data for this workform. You may have used Workform 3, Position Description Questionnaire (PDQ), or some other form to gather information on job duties and responsibilities from employees. Minimum job requirements data may come from PDQs and employee interviews, supervisor and management recommendations, or existing job descriptions.

Factors to Consider When Completing Workform 4

1. If discrepancies arise between an employee's description of her job and the supervisor's sense of the job, conduct additional interviews to determine actual job duties and responsibilities and the amount of time spent on the duties.

2. Take care in distinguishing between "essential functions" (those basic duties that are central to a job and cannot be transferred to another position without disruption in the flow or process of work) and "other functions" which might be performed in the job but are not essential.

3. Carefully consider the minimum job requirements. This is where you identify the knowledge, skills, and abilities of the job.

To Complete Workform 4

1. **Top of form.** Fill out each line with appropriate information. Position summary is a one- or two-sentence description of the purpose of the job.

2. **Section A.** List the essential function of the job, using the PDQ and interviews (if conducted) as the basis for the list.

3. **Section B.** List other major functions of the job, using the PDQ and interviews (if conducted) as the basis for the list.

4. **Section C.** For each job function, enter the estimated percentage of time spent on the function.

5. **Section D.** Fill out each minimum job requirement area. Complete the information at the bottom of the form:

   Completed by Enter the name of the person or persons who completed the workform.

   Source of data Indicate the source of the data used to complete the workform.

   Date completed Enter the date the workform was completed.

   Library Enter the library's name.

Factors to Consider When Reviewing Workform 4

Make sure all questions are answered and that specifics are provided for major job duties and responsibilities. If acronyms or library-specific terms are used, find out what they mean. Clarify any differences of opinion or emphasis between the employee's and the supervisor's view of the job.

JOB DESCRIPTION

Job title:	Salary range:	FLSA status:
Department:	Reports to:
Position summary:	

	C. Percentage of Time Spent on This Function
A. Essential Functions	
1.	%
2.	
3.	
4.	
5.	
B. Other Functions	
1.	
2.	
3.	

D. Minimum Job Requirements

Education:

Experience:

Specific skills and abilities:

Specialized knowledge, licenses, etc.:

Supervisory responsibility, if any:

Working conditions:

Completed by _____ Date completed _____

_____ Library

Source of data _____

Instructions

Purpose of Workform 5

Use this workform as a way to plan and manage your recruitment process.

Sources of Data for Workform 5

The data for your recruitment process plan and checklist will come from the job description you already have or will prepare for a new position and the processes already in place for recruiting new employees. If you don't have processes in place, this workform will provide a process for you to follow.

Factors to Consider When Completing Workform 5

1. Depending on the position to be filled, your recruitment schedule and approaches may vary.

2. Find out what paperwork requirements there are for your library or parent jurisdiction. These requirements may also include time lines and recommendations or requirements for the approaches you can take and the money you can spend on recruitment activities.

3. Take the time to carefully consider what knowledge, skills, and abilities and competencies you need. What do you want this position to accomplish? The job description you've written for the position should answer this question.

4. Position announcements, both internal and external, are often a brief paragraph or two. Supplement this brief announcement with a longer, more detailed announcement and/or brochure describing the job, the library and community, and the desired background, knowledge, skills, and abilities.

5. Supplemental questions are sometimes developed for professional, technical, and managerial-level positions. Determine if they will be needed. If so, write questions that reflect job requirements for the position and that will directly link with the job description.

To Complete Workform 5

1. **Position.** Indicate name of position being recruited for.

2. **Type of position.** Indicate whether the position will be full-time, part-time, hourly, contract, or some other type of position.

3. **Responsibility.** Indicate who or what group will be responsible for each step in the recruitment process. It may be the responsibility of an HR office or specialist, the hiring manager, or a library work group or team to handle a particular step in the process.

4. **Check if completed.** Check off each step in the process as complete. Indicate "N/A" if it's not applicable to a particular recruitment.

5. **Describe position to be filled.** Determine that you have described the position being recruited for as completely as possible by identifying what you want the person in the position to accomplish.

6. **Revise or write job description.** Determine whether or not an up-to-date job description exists for the position. If not, revise or write one, making sure it reflects job duties and responsibilities and needed KSAs.

7. **Fill out required paperwork.** Note whether paperwork required to begin the recruitment process has been completed.

8. **Plan recruitment schedule.** Develop the time line for all steps of the recruitment process. You may want to work backward from the date you hope to have the person starting work in the position.

9. **Determine where you will post job announcement.** Indicate that you have made advertising decisions that include the number of announcements or ads, whether internal, external, or both, and where you will place the announcements.

10. **Create job announcement.** Note that you have completed this step. There may be multiple announcements, depending on the recruitment strategy and time line selected.

11. **Create position brochure.** You may or may not do this step, depending on the position and your time line.

12. **Determine if supplemental questions will be part of the application process.** If you've decided to use supplemental questions, indicate that you've written the questions.

13. **Encourage employees to notify others.** Note that you have used various mechanisms (intranet, memo, general announcement) to make current employees aware of the job opening and to ask them to pass that information along to others they know who might be good candidates for the position.

14. **Attend job fairs, conferences, etc.** If time permits and it is part of the strategy for a particular position, note attendance at job fairs and conferences and/or networking contacts made.

Indicate "NA" if any of the steps are not applicable.
Complete the information at the bottom of the form:

Completed by Enter the name of the person or persons who completed the workform.

Source of data Indicate the source of the data used to complete the workform.

Date completed Enter the date the workform was completed.

Library Enter the library's name.

Factors to Consider When Reviewing Workform 5

This workform provides a process outline and checklist to use. The main factor to consider is whether or not you've assigned responsibility for and completed each step essential to a particular recruitment.

1. Position _____   Location _____

2. Full-time/Part-time/Hourly/Contract/Other (circle which applies)

	3. Responsibility of:	4. Date Started	5. Date Completed	6. Check When Completed
7. Describe position to be filled: KSAs, competencies, what you expect person in position to accomplish.				
8. Revise or write job description, if required.				
9. Fill out any required paperwork (personnel requisition, etc.) and obtain required approvals.				
10. Plan recruitment schedule, including scope, timetable, and selection techniques.				
11. Determine where you will post job announcement (internal bulletin board or intranet, newspapers, professional journals, e-mail lists, job boards, the library website, etc.) for the position.				
12. Create job announcement. If using multiple resources, tailor announcement to fit the resource being used.				
13. Depending on the position and recruitment strategy, create a position brochure.				
14. Determine if supplemental questions will be part of the application process. If so, develop and distribute with application materials.				
15. Encourage employees to inform family members, friends, and colleagues about the available position.				
16. If timetable makes it feasible and depending on position, attend and recruit at job fairs and professional conferences, distributing job announcement and/or brochure. Network with professional colleagues through e-mail, phone calls, and personal contacts.				

Completed by _____   Date completed _____

Source of data _____   Library _____

127

Instructions

Purpose of Workform 6

Use this form to develop questions to use during candidate interviews.

Sources of Data for Workform 6

Consider the types of questions you want to develop. Use information from the job description to develop performance-based and behavioral questions.

Factors to Consider When Completing Workform 6

1. The questions should be designed to uncover relevant facts about the candidate's educational, experience, and work background and to elicit information about what she has actually accomplished in her past positions.

2. Develop questions that link directly to the knowledge, skills, and abilities required of the job, behavioral competencies, and objectives identified in the job description. Remember to ask not just about what the candidate has (education, years of experience, etc.), but also about what the person has actually done with her education, experience, skills, etc., in past positions.

3. Remember that non-job-related questions cannot be asked. Examples of such questions include personal questions relating to marital status, child care responsibilities, languages spoken at home, racial or ethnic background, religious affiliation, disabilities, etc.

4. There is no need to have an equal number of questions of each type.

To Complete Workform 6

1. **Line A.** Write in the name of the position that the interview questions relate to.

2. **Column B.** This column lists the three major types of questions you could ask.

3. **Column C.** This column provides examples of each type of question. Use these examples as guides to developing your own questions.

4. **Column D.** Write in your own questions. While space is given for four of each type, you might develop a different number of each question, depending on the position you're filling and what you are looking for in the person you want to hire.

Complete the information at the bottom of the form:

Completed by Enter the name of the person or persons who completed the workform.

Source of data Indicate the source of the data used to complete the workform.

Date completed Enter the date the workform was completed.

Library Enter the library's name.

Factors to Consider When Reviewing Workform 6

Review your questions to be sure they will provide the information you need to make a hiring decision. You want to be sure that you know if the person being interviewed possesses the desired KSAs and what she has done with them in previous positions.

WORKFORM 6 Developing Interview Questions

A. Position: _____

B. Type of Question	C. Examples	D. Questions for This Position
Structured: Questions designed to elicit basic information	Can you tell me a little bit about yourself and your work background? What interests you about this job and what skills and strengths can you bring to it? Can you tell me about your current job? Can you describe a typical day in your current (or last) job? What size budget do you manage?	1. 2. 3. 4.
Performance-based: Questions designed to reveal actual work performance	Please think of the most significant accomplishment in your career (or work life). Please tell me all about it. [Ask follow-up questions to probe for details and specifics.] Please draw an organization chart and tell me about a team project you were involved in; describe your role. One of our key objectives for the person selected for this position is [describe objective from job description]. Please tell me about something similar you've accomplished. One major problem (or issue) we're now facing is [describe]. How would you go about addressing it? What would you need to know and how would you plan it out? What have you done that's most similar?	1. 2. 3. 4.
Behavioral: Questions designed to describe specific situations in past jobs that demonstrate behaviors key to open job	What three or four adjectives best describe your personality? Give me actual examples of when these traits have aided you in the performance of your job and when they have hurt. What sort of work environment do you prefer? What brings out your best performance? How do you handle conflict? Please give an example of how you handled a workplace conflict in the past. Tell me about a recent major directive of management that you had to communicate and implement. How did you go about doing this? Tell me about a situation where you had to solve a difficult problem. What did you do? What was your thought process? What was the outcome? What do you wish you had done differently? Working with people from diverse backgrounds or cultures can be a challenge. Can you tell me about a time you faced a challenge adapting to a person from a different background or culture? (What happened? What did you do? What was the result?)	1. 2. 3. 4.

Completed by _____   Date completed _____

Source of data _____   Library _____

To Complete Workform 7

Top lines

Fill out the top lines completely, so that you have a record of who you talked to and that person's title, organization, and contact information.

Questions

Ask each question and make note of the responses received. Ask follow-up questions to seek clarification and examples. Probe for specifics.

Factors to Consider When Reviewing Workform 7

1. Be sure that the reference has sufficient knowledge of the candidate's work performance that she can answer the questions accurately. Does the reference seem appropriate for the level of position that the candidate is applying for?

2. Probe for specifics. Don't be satisfied with generalities. Ask for work performance-related examples.

Instructions

Purpose of Workform 7

Use this workform to thoroughly check references. References are usually contacted by telephone. Don't simply send the form. You want to have interaction with the references.

Sources of Data for Workform 7

References provided by the candidate will be the source of data for the workform.

Factors to Consider When Completing Workform 7

1. Maintain a friendly but neutral demeanor when asking the questions. Don't lead the reference into providing the answers she thinks you want.

2. Select questions to be asked or how you use the form depending on the level of the position: you'll spend more time checking the references of a subject specialist librarian or manager than those of a clerk.

3. Take the time to thoroughly discuss the candidate's abilities and past performance with the reference. Don't hurry through the reference checking. Stay objective so that you hear both positive and negative comments.

REFERENCE CHECK FORM

(Verify that the applicant has provided permission before conducting reference checks)

Applicant's name: Date:

Position applying for: Position/Title of reference:

Person contacted: Phone no.

Organization:

Questions:

1. Would you serve as a reference? (This remains confidential)   Yes_____   No_____

2. When did this individual work for you?   From: To:

3. Explain the job and ask how they think the person would fit into the position. Use the job description in describing what you want the person to achieve in the job.

4. Please describe the job responsibilities or the type of work performed by the candidate:

5. How would you describe the applicant's relationships with coworkers, subordinates (if applicable), and superiors?

(Cont.)

131

6. Did the candidate have a positive or negative work attitude? Please elaborate.

7. How would you describe the quantity and quality of work output generated by the candidate?

8. Can you tell me about some of this individual's strengths and/or skills? (Remember to ask for examples)

9. What areas could this individual improve upon?

10. How would you characterize his/her work in general?

11. Would you recommend him/her for this position? Why or why not?

(Cont.)

12. Would you rehire this individual?   Yes _____   No _____   If no, why not?

Insert additional questions as required to assess the candidate's ability to meet performance objectives you've identified:

Thank you for your time and cooperation.

Completed by _____

Source of data _____

Date completed _____

Library _____

Instructions

Purpose of Workform 8

Use this form to plan individual activities for the performance period.

Who Should Complete Workform 8

This form should be completed by the employee and reviewed by the supervisor. Supervisors should provide support in completing this workform with new or recently promoted employees.

Sources of Data for Workform 8

Sources of data include the library's strategic plan, department work plan, and the job description for the employee's position.

In completing this form, ask:

- What are the library's priorities for the upcoming year?
- What are the department's priorities?
- How does this job contribute to the library and/or department meeting its goals?
- What are the activities that will need to be accomplished by this employee in order to move the library forward?
- What personal or professional developmental activities should be undertaken?
- What are the major functions, or basic work activities, that a person in this job must do regularly in order to be successful?
- What resources will be needed to complete the identified activities? Will the person in the job need support from another branch, unit, or department?

Factors to Consider When Completing Workform 8

The employee and supervisor should focus on the development of each activity in general, ensuring each is SMART and assessing the adequacy of training and resources.

1. Questions for each activity:
   - Does the activity support the library's and department's goals?
   - Is it measurable?
   - Is it results-oriented?
   - Is it supported by the needed authority and resources?
   - Is it challenging? Reasonable? Attainable?
   - Is it expressed in specific vs. general terms?

2. Make sure each activity is SMART:

   Specific Detail what needs to be done; this should not be vague or open to interpretation.

   Measurable Provide numbers, amount of change, percentage of change, etc.

   Achievable It should be a stretch, but achievable. Use action verbs like *create, build, lead, develop,* etc.

   Relevant Relate the activity to the library's and department's priorities; address library culture, context, environment, pace, resources available, policies, etc.

   Time-sensitive Indicate how long it will take, start to finish.

3. Ensure adequacy of resources:

   Ask: Does the employee have the knowledge, training, and resources to accomplish the activity? Does she have the authority? Is there enough:

   Time

   Fiscal resources

   Staff resources

   Training

   Authority

   Tools (technology, hardware, bookmobiles, etc., as appropriate)

To Complete Workform 8

1. **Line A**. Write in the name and position of the person completing the workform.
2. **Line B**. State the review or performance period covered by this workform.
3. **Column C**. List key activities for the upcoming year. (Note that activities may exceed one year. List milestones for activities that are long-term or have multiple milestones.)

(Cont.)

4. **Column D.** List the measures of success for the position. How will the supervisor and employee know if the activity has been accomplished? What will be different? At what cost? Over what period of time?

5. **Column E.** List the resources that the employee will need (if any) to accomplish the activity.

6. **Column F.** Enter the start and end (expected completion) dates of the activity. If it is ongoing, write "ongoing."

7. **Column G.** This column allows you to write any comments pertaining to the activity, including assumptions made about resources, etc.

If you need help with the definitions of any of these concepts, refer back to the text in chapter 5.

Complete the information at the bottom of the form:

> *Supervisor*   The supervisor should sign and date the workform.
>
> *Employee*   The employees should sign and date the workform.

Factors to Consider When Reviewing Workform 8

1. Ensure that all activities are either day-to-day or development; that they link to the library's ongoing or strategic goals; and that they are SMART.

2. If any of the activities are dependent on resources from another department, make sure that these are available.

3. For larger projects/goals, break up into phases or modules
   - Set a time limit for each phase.
   - Do progress checks as you go along to make sure phases are completed.

4. Attach additional sheets as necessary.

WORKFORM 8 Individual Performance Plan

A. Name of employee: _____ Position: _____

B. Performance period: From: _____ To: _____

C. **Activities** (in order of importance)	**D.** **Measures of Success**	**E.** **Resources Needed**	**F.** **Begin/End Date**	**G.** **Comments**
1.	• • •	• • •		
2.	• • •	• • •		
3.	• • •	• • •		
4.	• • •	• • •		
5.	• • •	• • •		
6.	• • •	• • •		

(Cont.)

C. Activities (in order of importance)	D. Measures of Success	E. Resources Needed	F. Begin/End Date	G. Comments
7.	• • •	• • •		
8.	• • •	• • •		

Employee: _____ Date _____

Supervisor: _____ Date _____

Completed by _____ Date completed _____

Source of data _____ Library _____

To Complete Workform 9

1. **Row A.** Complete this row at the beginning of the performance period. Write in the name and title of the person being evaluated, the supervisor's name and title, the dates of the review or performance period covered by this workform, and the date of the planning discussion. The employee should also sign in this row to indicate that the discussion took place and that the employee is in agreement with the activities and performance essentials as defined.

2. **Row B.** Complete this section when the required progress review has been completed (if the system requires such a review). The supervisor and employee both sign and date this section to indicate that the discussion took place.

3. **Rows C, D, and E.** Complete these sections if optional progress reviews have been completed (if the system includes such reviews). The supervisor and employee both sign and date this section to indicate that each discussion took place. Additional rows for optional progress reviews can be added if necessary.

4. **Section F.** This serves as a reference to define the performance rating levels available to the supervisor in rating the activities of the employee.

5. **Section G.** This section is used by the supervisor to rate each individual activity laid out by the employee and supervisor during performance planning or updated during the year.

6. **Column H.** Enter the activities from Workform 8, Individual Performance Plan, completed by employee and supervisor at the beginning of the performance period.

7. **Column I.** Enter the measures of success for the position for each activity from Workform 8.

8. **Column J.** Check the box indicating if the activity is basic work (B) or development (D).

9. **Column K.** Enter the rating for each activity, based on the employee's performance during the year in accomplishing the activity. Refer to the measures to ensure success was achieved.

10. **Column L.** Enter comments on each activity to provide the employee with specific, factual feedback.

11. **Section M.** Use this section to rate the employee on the performance of activities related to the performance essentials defined by the library. If the library chooses to use performance essentials, these categories of performance are included in the evaluations for all employees, though they may include additional categories for management staff.

(Cont.)

Instructions

Purpose of Workform 9

Use this form to evaluate the employee's performance for the entire performance period.

Who Should Complete Workform 9

This form should be completed by the supervisor and reviewed at the performance evaluation meeting with the employee.

Sources of Data for Workform 9

Sources of data include the employee's individual activity plan, the employee's self-evaluation (if used), the supervisor's coaching notes, the employee's job description, and the supervisor's general performance documentation for the employee from throughout the performance period.

In completing this form, ask:

- Did the employee successfully accomplish the day-to-day duties and responsibilities of the job description?

- Did the employee achieve each activity fully, as expected, on time and within budget (according to parameters)?

- Did library priorities shift during the year or period and cause the employee's activities to change? If so, did the employee successfully accomplish the newly identified activities?

- Has the employee met the library's performance essentials as defined (if applicable in your system)?

- Have you provided comments and examples of the employee's performance, using facts, not conclusions, opinions, or guesses about motivation?

Factors to Consider When Completing Workform 9

Supervisors and managers should be prepared for each performance evaluation meeting. Supervisors should review the employee's activities and actual performance. The self-evaluation should also be reviewed (if used) prior to the evaluation meeting. Supervisors should refamiliarize themselves with coaching notes and documentation and think about employee's objections to less than stellar ratings. Think about responses and rehearse dialogue. Supervisors should review and understand potential performance-rating errors and review comments and feedback to ensure these types of errors are not present. Finally, supervisors should have activities prepared for discussion regarding the next performance cycle.

WORKFORM 9 **Performance Evaluation Tool** *Instructions* (Cont.)

12. **Column N.** This defines the performance category or performance essential.

13. **Column O.** Enter the activities agreed upon by the supervisor and employee during performance planning that relate to each category.

14. **Column P.** Check the box indicating if the activity is basic work (B) or development (D).

15. **Column Q.** Enter the rating for each activity, based on the employee's performance during the year in accomplishing the activity. Refer to the definitions of the performance category as necessary.

16. **Column R.** Enter comments on each activity to provide the employee with specific, factual feedback.

17. **Section S.** Enter the overall rating for the employee during the performance period, in consideration of the ratings on individual activities and performance essential categories.

18. **Section T.** Enter comments on the overall performance of the employee during the performance period. Make sure to avoid rating errors and to provide factual, useful, and specific feedback the employee can use to improve or reinforce performance.

19. **Section U.** Employee comments.

20. **Section V.** Check one box to indicate if the job description for the position is up-to-date or has changed. If the job description has changed, revise and attach an updated job description.

21. **Section W.** Complete the information at the bottom of the form. Both the supervisor and employee should sign and date the form, indicating the date of the discussion. There is also a space for a second reviewer's signature. Use this space if the library has department heads or the director review the completed evaluation forms.

If you need help with the definitions of any of these concepts, refer back to the text in chapter 5.

Factors to Consider When Reviewing Workform 9

1. Ensure that the supervisor has familiarized herself with common rating errors and provides factual and specific feedback to the employee.

2. Review and consider the employee's self-evaluation (if used) in completing the evaluation form.

3. Provide comments and feedback in each section (positive or constructive) in order to facilitate improved performance or to reinforce outstanding performance.

4. Attach additional sheets as necessary.

PERFORMANCE EVALUATION

A. Performance Planning

(complete at the beginning of the performance period)

Employee Name: _____ Position Title: _____

Supervisor Name: _____ Department: _____

Performance Period: From _____ To _____ Performance Planning Discussion Date: _____

Employee Signature:* _____

* Indicates that employee agrees to work toward meeting these activities and performance essentials

B. Progress Review: Required

(one review required midway through the performance period)

Supervisor Signature: _____ Discussion Date: _____

Employee Signature: ** _____

** Indicates only that this discussion between employee and supervisor was held

C. Optional Progress Review

Supervisor Signature: _____ Discussion Date: _____

Employee Signature: ** _____

** Indicates only that this discussion between employee and supervisor was held

(Cont.)

D. Optional Progress Review

Discussion Date: _____

Supervisor Signature: _____

Employee Signature: ** _____

** Indicates only that this discussion between employee and supervisor was held

E. Optional Progress Review

Discussion Date: _____

Supervisor Signature: _____

Employee Signature: ** _____

** Indicates only that this discussion between employee and supervisor was held

Expand as necessary with additional progress checks.

(Cont.)

F. Performance Rating

(Rate by Category)

3 Outstanding	2 Fully Successful	1 Needs Improvement

G. Individual Activities

H. Activity	I. Measurements	J. ☐ B ☐ D Activity	K. ☐ 3 ☐ 2 ☐ 1 Results	L. Comments
1.				
2.				
3.				
4.				

(Cont.)

M. Performance Essentials

N. Performance Category Measures	O. Measures	P. □ B □ D Activity	Q. □ 3 □ 2 □ 1 Results	R. Details/Comments
Job Knowledge Understands and executes job duties, processes, and/or procedures. Uses ingenuity and skills to continuously review and identify internal departmental process improvements.	1. 2. 3.			
Quality/Productivity Work is done on time yet fairly, accurately, completely, and in accordance with established procedures. Does not sacrifice quality for speed, etc.	1. 2. 3.			
Customer Service Responsive to external as well as internal customers. Has the ability to maintain customer confidence and trust. Is able to get positive results in adverse situations.	1. 2. 3.			
Managerial Effectiveness *(If applicable)* Creates and achieves a desired future through influence on organizational values, individual and group goals, and processes and procedures. Consider how well the employee coaches and develops subordinates.	1. 2. 3.			

(Cont.)

Evaluation

S. Rating:

T. Supervisor Comments:

U. Employee Comments:

V. Please check one:

☐ The job description is up-to-date.

☐ The job has changed. An updated job description is attached.

W. Performance Evaluation

(complete at the end of the performance period)

Supervisor Signature: _____   Date: _____

Second Reviewer Signature: _____   Date: _____

Employee Signature: ***

Discussion Date: _____

*** Indicates only that this evaluation was reviewed with employee

Completed by _____   Date completed _____

Source of data _____   Library _____

Instructions

Purpose of Workform 10

Use this form to allow employees to provide feedback on their own performance.

Who Should Complete Workform 10

The workform should be completed by employees preparing for their annual performance evaluation meeting. Employees should submit the completed self-evaluation to their supervisor prior to the evaluation meeting within the time frame set forth by the library.

Sources of Data for Workform 10

Sources of data include the employee's own notes and documentation on her performance throughout the year.

Factors to Consider When Completing Workform 10

Encourage employees to think about their entire year's performance—not just recent events. Some employees keep a notebook to jot down key happenings or milestones in order to remember them when preparing for the evaluation meeting. Alternatively, employees can keep a copy of this document in their computer in order to keep a running file on the year's activities.

To Complete Workform 10

1. **Section A.** The employee answers the questions relating to her perspective on her performance during the current performance period. She can refer to notes kept on her performance throughout the year, or attach documents, certificates, or other attachments that will be useful in answering the questions.

2. **Section B.** The employee answers the questions relating to the upcoming performance period. She should refer to the accomplishments or areas for improvement in the current performance year in determining the areas of focus and planning for the upcoming year.

Factors to Consider When Reviewing Workform 10

Ensure the questions about the current performance year take the entire year into consideration vs. recent events only.

Think about the resources and support that will be necessary to accomplish the items listed in answer to the questions in Section B. Be as specific as possible so that these can be included in Workform 8, Individual Performance Plan, for the upcoming year.

SELF-EVALUATION

Two weeks before the end of the performance period, please reflect on the year and respond to the following questions. It may also be helpful to keep notes or a journal of your accomplishments during the year so that you can refer back to them at the end of the performance period.

A. Current Performance Period

1. Of what accomplishments and skills acquired during this performance period are you particularly proud?

2. What areas of your work do you believe need strengthening?

3. What were you expected to do, what did you do, and what else did you do?

B. Upcoming Performance Period

1. What can be done to make you more effective in your job?

2. What can be done to help you provide better service to your customers (internal and external)?

3. How can your supervisor or others help your succeed?

4. What are your career goals for the next three years? Five years? Are they compatible with the library's strategy?

5. What competencies and skills will you need to build to be ready for these goals?

6. What developmental activities would be helpful to you in building these skills and competencies?

period, please reflect upon the year and respond to the following. It may also be helpful to keep notes or a journal of your accomplishments during the year so that you may refer back to them at the end of the performance period.

Please expand as necessary.

Completed by _____ Date completed _____

Source of data _____ Library _____

Instructions

Purpose of Workform 11

Use this workform to develop or revamp an employee orientation program and plan for the success of new hires.

Sources of Data for Workform 11

Sources of data include your understanding and knowledge of staff and procedures, feedback from new hires and current employees, and personnel policies and procedures.

Factors to Consider When Completing Workform 11

1. Other library staff will be involved in this process, so be sure to plan in advance and coordinate their schedules.

2. Assign one person to manage the orientation process. This may be someone from your human resources department or a librarian or other person knowledgeable and skilled in adult learning and HR policies.

3. Except for item 6, the outline of an orientation program, this workform should be started by the hiring manager as soon as the new employee has accepted the library's offer of employment.

4. Spend time during the orientation on customer service (item 6c). Don't just state the library's policies. Give examples, ask employees about good and bad customer service, ask them to role play a variety of situations, share experiences (both as a customer and a provider), etc. The orientation is a wonderful opportunity to begin to acculturate new hires into their role as a leader in providing excellent service to all customers.

WORKFORM 11 New Employee Orientation

To Complete Workform 11

1. **Column A.** Review the action items and outline for an orientation program.
2. **Column B.** Note the person who is responsible.
3. **Column C.** Note the due date.

Factors to Consider When Reviewing Workform 11

1. Developing the basic orientation program will be easier if the library has a written employee handbook that includes policies and procedures. If it doesn't have policies all in one place, they will need to be gathered and summarized.

2. The orientation program can take place in one-half-day blocks over a period of time to help avoid information overload.

3. The orientation program should be fun and interactive. Several people should be involved in conducting it, even if they visit for only a short time, e.g., to talk about the library's history and strategic plan, or about their department or service (e.g., children's programming or circulation) or program (e.g., the employee assistance program).

4. The orientation program should not be boring or overwhelming. Remember that employees can absorb only so much at a time.

5. Ask the library director to attend the orientation program, even just for a few minutes, to welcome new employees.

A. New hire (name): _____

B. Position: _____

C. Supervisor: _____

D. Staff member tasked with responsibility for the New Hire Orientation Plan: _____

Date of hire: _____

Department: _____

A. Actions That Will Ensure Success of New Hires	**B.** Who Is Responsible	**C.** Date Due

1. Before the first day of work:
  a. Send the employee an agenda of the orientation program.
  b. Stay in touch with the employee to answer questions or provide other assistance.
  c. Prepare the work area, including space, desk, computer, and telephone.
  d. Let staff know that the employee will be starting; encourage coworkers to stop by and say hello.
  e. Develop FAQs that will help the employee get jump-started.		

2. Get the paperwork (hiring and insurance forms) out of the way even before the employee's first day.		
3. If new to the area, help the employee get settled.		
4. Make the employee's first day welcoming. Have balloons; breakfast/lunch to introduce her to her colleagues; ask the library director to stop by. Create a positive experience.		

5. Start orientation with the basics: what the employee needs to know to get through the first week(s) of work.
  a. Location of restrooms; work hours, lunch and break periods; use of staff lounge
  b. Procedures if employee needs to be late for work or leave early
  c. Parking, transportation
  d. Pay; including payday, procedures for submitting time cards; when and how paychecks are be distributed
  e. Dress
  f. Use of telephone and equipment; e-mail
  g. Emergency procedures
  h. Provide employee handbook		

(Cont.)

148

WORKFORM 11 **New Employee Orientation** (cont.)

A. Actions That Will Ensure Success of New Hires	B. Who Is Responsible	C. Date due

6. Contents of the orientation program should include
 	
  a. History and goals of library; governance; organizational structure; vision and values of the library; ethics
 	
  b. Working for a government organization, merit system, role of the board of trustees
 	
  c. Customer service in the library
 	
  d. Career development, continuing education; tuition assistance; promotions and transfers, performance management
 	
  f. The role of the union
 	
  g. EAP (employee assistance program)
 	
  h. Safety, including worker's compensation
 	
  i. Pay and benefits
 	
  j. Other:
 	
Note: You could follow your employee handbook and highlight key areas.		

7. Ask for feedback about the orientation program in a consistent way (provide a form). Use the data and make changes.		
8. Assign a buddy or mentor.		
9. Ensure that managers know that successful orientation is *their* responsibility.		
10. Follow up with the new hire. Check in after 30/60/90 days. Respond to employee's needs and concerns. Make changes to the orientation as appropriate.		
11. Other:		

Completed by _____ Date completed _____

Source of data _____ Library _____

Instructions

WORKFORM 12 Exit Interview Questionnaire

Purpose of Workform 12

Use this workform to interview employees who have resigned their positions. This will broaden your understanding of how employees see your library.

Sources of Data for Workform 12

This is strictly employee opinions, thoughts, and feelings.

Factors to Consider When Completing Workform 12

1. Let the employee know that the answers she provides are confidential and the purpose of the exit interview is to learn about her experiences with the goal of making improvements.

2. Allow the employee to say whatever she chooses to share.

3. Do not engage the employee in debate or try to counter her opinions.

4. Do not take what is said personally.

5. Prepare follow-up questions and probe gently if the employee is providing superficial answers.

To Complete Workform 12

Section A. Fill in the relevant information.

Section B. Fill in employee opinions.

Questions 1–8. Ask the employee these questions.

Questions 9+. Ask other questions that are relevant to your library.

Question 13. Ask the employee for any other comments she might have.

Question 16. This is the space for interviewer comments, thoughts, and observations.

Factors to Consider When Reviewing Workform 12

1. How will this data be reported without breaking confidentiality? To whom will it be reported?

2. What will you do with the data?

3. Keep in mind the context of the information you are receiving. Did the employee have "an ax to grind"?

EMPLOYEE EXIT INTERVIEW

Section A

A. Employee name:

Position: $Pay:

B. Date of hire:

Last day of work:

C. Initial position:

Final position:

Section B

1. Why are you leaving your job as a _____ at the Library?

2. Did it (the new job) find you or did you find it?

3. If you are going to another job, what does that job offer that your job here did not?

4. What factors contributed to your accepting a job here? Were your expectations met?

5. How would you evaluate your current salary and benefits at the Library? How do these compare to your salary and benefits in your new job?

6. How would you describe your working relationship with your supervisor?

7. How would you describe the working relationships you had with members of your branch/unit/department and other members of the staff?

(Cont.)

Section B

8. Did your work fulfill you? Give you a sense of accomplishment? Was it challenging?
9. What could the Library have done to make the job more fulfilling or challenging?
10. Did you feel you had opportunities to expand your knowledge and learning?
11. What knowledge, skills, and abilities do you feel were required to do your job, and did you have them?
12. What did you like best about working at the Library? What did you not like?
13. What comments or suggestions do you have that will help us make the Library an even better place to work?
14. Would you recommend the Library to a friend as a place to work? If yes, why? If no, why not?
15. If there was an opportunity to return, would you?
16. Other comments

Expand as necessary

Completed by _____   Date completed _____

Source of data _____   Library _____

Index

Jeanne Goodrich is a consultant and trainer who specializes in public library planning, work and workflow analysis, and data collection and analysis. Before going into consulting full-time, she was deputy director of the Multnomah County Library in Portland, Oregon. She has more than thirty-five years of experience in public library management, including directing medium-sized libraries and serving as deputy director for library development at a state library agency. She is the coauthor of *Staffing for Results: A Guide to Working Smarter* (2002).

Paula M. Singer is the principal consultant of The Singer Group, Inc., a firm specializing in compensation, leadership and human resources development, strategic planning, succession planning, and organization design. She has more than twenty years of experience as a consultant. She also teaches graduate classes in organization development and strategic human resources at Johns Hopkins University. Singer is the author of *Developing a Compensation Plan for Your Library* (2002) and a coauthor of *Winning with Library Leadership: Enhancing Services through Connection, Contribution, and Collaboration* (2004) and *Best Practices in Learning and Development* (2002).